CONSTITUTION
VS
GUERRIERE

Frigates during the War of 1812

MARK LARDAS

First published in Great Britain in 2009 by Osprey Publishing,
Midland House, West Way, Botley, Oxford OX2 0PH, UK
443 Park Avenue South, New York, NY 10016, USA
E-mail: info@ospreypublishing.com

A CIP catalog record for this book is available from the British Library

Print ISBN 978 1 84603 434 3
PDF e-book ISBN 978 1 84908 094 1

Page layout by: Ken Vail Graphic Design, Cambridge, UK
Maps by Peter Bull Art Studio
Index by Michael Forder
Typeset in ITC Conduit and Adobe Garamond
Originated by PDQ Digital Media Solutions
Printed in China through Bookbuilders
09 10 11 12 13   10 9 8 7 6 5 4 3 2 1

Osprey Publishing is supporting the Woodland Trust, the UK's leading woodland
conservation charity, by funding the dedication of trees.

Artist's note

Readers may care to note that the original paintings from
which the battlescene and cover artwork in this book were
prepared are available for private sale. All reproduction
copyright whatsoever is retained by the Publishers. All
inquiries should be addressed to:

Giuseppe Rava
Via Borgotto 17
48018 Faenza (RA)
Italy

giuseppe.rava@fastwebnet.it

The Publishers regret that they can enter into no
correspondence upon this matter.

Author's note:

The following abbreviations indicate the sources of the
illustrations used in this volume:

FDRL – Franklin Delano Roosevelt Presidential Library
Collection

LOC – Library of Congress, Washington, DC

USNHF – United States Navy Historical Foundation,
Washington DC

USNAM – United States Naval Academy Museum

AC – Author's Collection

Other sources are listed in full.

Dedication:

This book is dedicated to Bruce Biskup, a co-worker,
modeler, wargamer and friend.

FOR A CATALOGUE OF ALL BOOKS PUBLISHED BY OSPREY
MILITARY AND AVIATION PLEASE CONTACT:

Osprey Direct, c/o Random House Distribution Center,
400 Hahn Road, Westminster, MD 21157
Email: uscustomerservice@ospreypublishing.com

Osprey Direct, The Book Service Ltd, Distribution Centre,
Colchester Road, Frating Green, Colchester, Essex, CO7 7DW
E-mail: customerservice@ospreypublishing.com

www.ospreypublishing.com

CONTENTS

INTRODUCTION

Command of a frigate was the goal of every dashing captain during the Age of Fighting Sail, the period from 1650 through 1820. Not only could a frigate beat anything that it could catch and escape from anything that could beat it, but the captain of a frigate also commanded the most potent independent warship afloat. A ship of the line, though larger and more powerful, usually operated in a squadron under an admiral's command, and fought under his directions in a rigid line of battle. Sloops of war or corvettes were lighter than frigates, and were easy prey for the big cruisers. The various smaller craft – such as cutters, luggers, and schooners – were used either as dispatch ships or convoy escorts, and were commanded by junior officers. For a captain hungry for distinction, a frigate command was the pinnacle.

Attached to a fleet, a frigate operated as a scout, probing independently for the enemy. Frigates also served individually or in small squadrons as cruisers, hunting out the enemy's merchant ships, lone warships and privateers. These commands were made more desirable by the existence of prize money, by which the value of captured enemy ships and cargoes was paid out to captains, officers and crew in fixed proportions. With the riches of the world's trade still carried by sea, a successful cruise could make a ship's company rich.

But a frigate command offered a captain something even harder to achieve than wealth. In an age that revered its fighting men, particularly those who fought according to a gentleman's code of honor, a victorious frigate duel could make a captain a figure of international renown. Even losing a single-ship action could make a captain a national hero, if his conduct was admirable enough. Richard Pearson was knighted following his spirited defense of HMS *Serapis*, despite his loss to the *Bonhomme Richard*.

Captains would occasionally go to extremes to arrange a duel with an opposite number. More than once, captains sent written challenges to a rival, in the manner of gentlemen fighting a personal duel rather than a battle between two national warships. On occasion, other ships in a blockading squadron were sent away to ensure that two ships could fight without interference.

Rituals of combat evolved. A ship indicated its willingness to fight by backing sail, to allow an opponent upwind to reach it. Both ships cleared for action, removing furniture, partitions, and unnecessary items to the holds. The gundecks were left bare of everything except the guns and the men who served them. Once a commander saw no choice but to surrender his ship, he ordered his colors to be lowered. The victor

Big, bluff Isaac Hull was one of the US Navy's more junior captains in the War of 1812. This painting shows him as a young captain, as he would have appeared at the time. (USNHF)

would wait on his quarterdeck, sending a lieutenant to accept his opponent's surrender. As a token of submission, the vanquished officers would offer their swords to the victors. In recognition of a hard fight, the victor would often chivalrously refuse the sword, offer his commissioned opponents the hospitality of the wardroom, and parole.

This tradition never shone brighter than during the War of 1812. The two nations spoke the same language, and shared a common history. The opposing captains knew each other, often through long acquaintance during the years of peace. Both sides were eager to test their skill against the other, and both sides were supremely confident of victory. And since glory, more than gold, was the coin of the officer class of both navies, both sides actively sought opportunities to fight.

But under the mystique, the reality was rather grimmer. A frigate crammed between 250 and 500 men into an area not much bigger than a basketball court, and in combat the ships hurled 18lb to 42lb solid iron balls at each other, with enough force to smash through several feet of solid oak. A hit sent lethal shards of jagged hardwood flying through the cramped decks. In combat, sailors could get crushed by the vicious recoil of their own guns, or crushed by a block or spar sent crashing to the deck by cannon fire. An injured sailor could expect only rudimentary medical treatment. Amputation was common, and antisepsis unknown.

The butcher's bill – as the casualty figures were known – for a hard-fought frigate duel was usually high. A victorious frigate often lost between ten and 25 percent of

There was a protocol for every aspect of a frigate duel, including surrender. The defeated captain was to go to the victor, and surrender his sword. This print supposedly illustrates Isaac Hull receiving James Dacres' sword. Since Dacres was badly injured during the battle, this illustration is romance rather than history. (AC)

its crew, and a casualty rate of 25 percent was usually the minimum that a losing frigate could expect. Often, casualties were divided like prize money: the lion's share went to the officers. Crews knew that leadership decided battles, and worked to deprive their enemy of its leaders. Not only were they valuable targets, but as the only uniformed men on the ship, the officers made obvious targets for marksmen.

Yet for the fame and mystique that surrounded these encounters, frigate battles often failed to serve any national interests. In chasing the glory of dueling with an enemy warship, captains often neglected their original mission. In many cases, battle damage forced victorious American frigates back to ports that they had spent months trying to leave, keeping them from their important role of harrying Britain's maritime trade. On the other side, British captains frequently sought to engage the big American frigates alone, even when it was both possible and prudent to keep the enemy under observation until assistance arrived. In both cases, winning a war took second place to personal honor.

Despite, or perhaps because of these contradictions, the single-ship duel continues to hold a unique appeal. For hundreds of years and in many forms, single combat has often been seen as the chivalrous ideal of warfare. And the classic frigate battle was a single combat writ large.

Following the American victories in 1812, the British Admiralty ordered several frigates using the lines of HMS *Endymion*, a frigate intended to carry a 24-pounder main battery. HMS *Glasgow* was the first of these five frigates to be ordered, and the last one commissioned. It had a short career, being broken up in 1829. (AC)

CHRONOLOGY

1793
January 21   Revolutionary France declares war on Britain, beginning two decades of conflict.

1794
March 24   The United States authorizes a navy: headed by six heavy frigates including *Constitution*, *United States*, and *Chesapeake*.

1797
May 10   USS *United States* launched.
October 21   USS *Constitution* launched.

1799
December 10   USS *Chesapeake* launched.

1798–1800
   Quasi-War with France: Britain and the United States are allies.

1802
March 25   Peace of Amiens established between Britain and France.

1803
May 22   War between France and Britain resumes.

1805
October 21   Battle of Trafalgar.

Whether your side won or lost, a hard-fought frigate duel could serve as inspiration. When Oliver Hazard Perry sailed against the British fleet at the battle of Lake Erie, his flagship *Lawrence* flew a banner with James Lawrence's dying words, "Don't give up the ship." (LOC)

1806
July 19   Royal Navy captures *Guerrière* (launched 1799).
August 3   HMS *Shannon* launched.

1807
June 22   *Chesapeake–Leopard* incident.

The fruits of glory: a dress sword, presented to Captain Stephen Decatur by the city of Philadelphia for his victory over HMS *Macedonian*. Such tokens were a common reward for a captain victorious in a frigate duel. (USNAM)

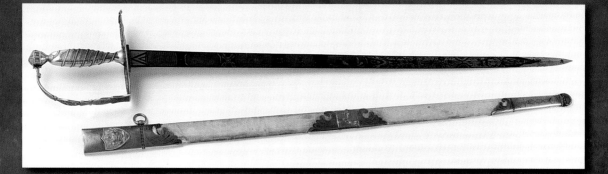

1810

June 6 HMS *Macedonian* launched.

1811

May 16 *Little Belt* affair.

May 20 HMS *Java*, then French *Renommée* (launched 1805) captured.

1812

June 18 United States declares war on Britain.

July 17–18 British squadron chases *Constitution*.

August 19 *Constitution* defeats *Guerrière*.

October 30 *United States* captures *Macedonian*.

December 29 *Constitution* meets and defeats *Java*.

1813

February 24 USS *Hornet* fights and sinks HMS *Peacock*.

May 20 James Lawrence takes command of *Chesapeake*.

June 1 *Chesapeake* sails from Boston harbor to meet *Shannon*. In a 15-minute battle *Chesapeake* is taken as a prize.

1814

March 28 USS *Essex* is captured at Valparaiso by two British frigates.

December 24 Treaty of Ghent signed.

1815

January 15 USS *President* captured by a British squadron attempting to escape New York harbor.

February 17 US Congress ratifies Treaty of Ghent, ending War of 1812.

February 20 *Constitution* fights and captures HMS *Cyane* and *Levant* off the Azores.

The battle between the *Chesapeake* and *Shannon* was perhaps the bloodiest quarter-hour of battle during the entire Age of Sail. In just 15 minutes one-third of all participants became casualties. (USNHF)

DESIGN AND DEVELOPMENT

THE FRIGATE

The classic sailing frigate was a three-masted, square-rigged warship, mounting its main armament of cannon on a single gun deck. Originally a French innovation, as were many aspects of sailing ship design, frigates first appeared in the late 1730s, and grew heavier and more powerful throughout the eighteenth century. The British captured several early French frigates during the Seven Years' War (1756–63) and soon started building their own. By the middle of the eighteenth century, every navy was building frigates.

The single-deck frigate filled the role formerly played by the previous generation of medium-sized cruisers, which carried 30 to 56 guns on two gun decks and were known as two-deckers, Both types were intended as powerful scouts, raiders and convoy escorts. Neither was able to fight ships of the line, which were intended to fight in line of battle against other fleets, and which in the early eighteenth century were armed with between 64 and 100 guns.

Frigates had several advantages over the two-deckers they replaced. In these earlier cruisers, the lower deck, where the crew slept, was also the main gun deck. The extra weight of two banks of guns meant that the gun ports on the lower deck had to be dangerously low – only 2ft to 3ft above the waterline. That meant that these guns were unusable in even moderate seas. Stability issues meant that the guns carried on the upper deck had to be smaller – and lighter – than the lower deck guns.

By moving the guns previously carried on the lower deck to the upper deck, a more seaworthy design emerged. The lower deck, free of guns, could be set closer to the waterline. In turn, this meant the upper deck, where the main battery was now located, could be lower, which reduced the height of the ship's upper works. This made it better under sail since, as a ship's bulwarks catch the wind, a ship with tall sides had to fight wind as well as water to gain speed.

At between 5ft and 7ft above the waterline, the frigate's main battery was significantly higher than that of the old two-deckers it replaced, allowing a frigate to use its main guns whatever the weather, unless the weather was so bad that no ship could fight. Although its battery might be smaller than that of a two-decker, its guns would be at least as heavy, and additional guns could be mounted on the upper works where previously none could be carried. As an added benefit, clearing the lower deck of guns gave the crews more space, which increased the livability of a frigate. Since a frigate required a smaller crew and boasted more storage, it could remain unsupplied at sea longer.

The move toward frigates also conserved manpower. A two-decker took 350 men. A frigate with comparable firepower could be manned with 300 men, and lighter frigates carried crews of between 200 and 280 men. Nations with large navies could thus commission a fleet with more firepower for the same number of men.

Broadly speaking, the first generation of frigates was smaller than those built after 1800. A keel of just over 100ft was typical, which yielded a gun deck that was between 125ft and 135ft in length. Often these ships were pierced for 11 guns on a side on the main deck, but with only ten guns actually mounted. The first frigates typically carried 9-pounder long guns on the main deck, with 3- or 4-pounder long guns on the forecastle and quarterdeck.

A frigate had two complete decks, and partial decks above and below these, with its main battery of guns mounted on the upper or main deck. Below the main deck

Frigates used the lower deck exclusively as crew quarters, whereas in previous two-decker cruisers this cramped space also served as a gun deck. This allowed a frigate to carry a heavier battery on the upper deck, at a greater height above the water. Not sharing hammock space with either guns or hawse-holes also made living conditions healthier. (AC)

was the lower or berth deck, where the crew slept, and which was still above the waterline. Beneath the berth deck was the orlop. Made up of platforms, the orlop was primarily used for storage and to house a frigate's junior warrant officers. The anchor cables were stowed at this level, ahead of the mainmast, in the cable tier. Under the orlop was the hold, where casks of food, water, supplies and firewood were stowed.

Above the gun deck were the forecastle and quarterdeck. Originally raised platforms at the bow and stern, by the eighteenth century they had become additional part-decks, integral to the hull, which improved a ship's ability to weather high seas and aided in handling the ship. The ship was commanded from the quarterdeck at the stern, where the ship's wheel lay and where the captain, master, and first lieutenant were stationed. By the 1790s, the forecastle and quarterdeck were linked with gangways that allowed crew to go directly from one to the other. By 1812, these gangways had become substantial. On US Navy frigates it was the custom to call these linked decks the spar deck.

Frigates easily outsailed the old two-deckers, and could sail as fast as lighter ships, such as brigs and sloops, except in calm winds. They could also expect to outsail ships of the line, except in stormy conditions, when the extra mass and sail height of the ship of the line told in its favor. Such weather could even the odds though, as a ship of the line would place itself in danger if it opened its lower gun ports to the high seas. Under these conditions, a frigate could defeat a ship of the line, though such a victory occurred only once in the frigate era, when the frigates HMS *Indefatigable* and HMS *Amazon* fought the French 74-gun *Droits de l'Homme*. Fought in a full gale off a lee shore, it ended with *Amazon* and *Droits de l'Homme* driven ashore, and *Indefatigable* the lone survivor.

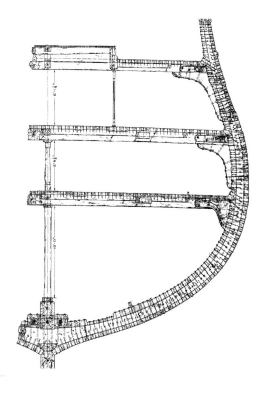

Cross-section of *Constitution*, amidships. From top to bottom: spar deck, gun deck, berth deck, and hold. Amidships, the spar deck had a large opening to the gun deck, and was spanned by two broad gangways. The orlop would be approximately 5ft below the berth deck. It was not a complete deck, and one of the breaks was amidships, to facilitate hold stowage. (US Navy)

Ships of this era were armed with smoothbore, muzzle-loading cannon, which fired solid iron shot, and were rated by the weight of the ball fired. As the damage inflicted by a shot increased non-linearly – a 12lb shot did significantly more damage than two 6lb shot striking the same object – navies were keen to mount the heaviest guns that they could. The biggest guns carried at sea in this era typically fired a 32lb ball, which was the heaviest shot that could comfortably be carried by one man on the deck of a pitching and heaving ship. Guns firing heavier shot, 42lb or 68lb in weight, were occasionally carried, but these very heavy guns were mostly carronades rather than long guns. However, the weight of the shot made them tricky to manage.

Ships of the line were typically armed with 32-pounder or 24-pounder cannon on their lower decks, and 18-pounder or 24-pounder cannon on their upper decks. Sloops of war, brigs of war and corvettes, which were smaller single-decked warships, carried a main battery of 3-pounder to 9-pounder cannon. Thus, a frigate had rough firepower parity with a ship of the line that could only use its upper battery, while it could

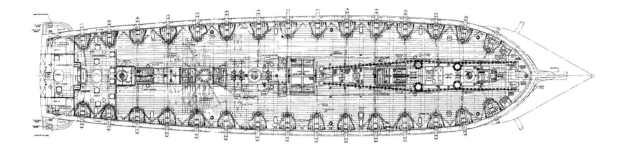

overpower any smaller warship. This combination of speed and firepower made frigates ideal ships to use as scouts, for convoy protection, and as commerce raiders.

A 24-gun frigate, typical of the mid-eighteenth century, might have a main battery of 18 9-pounders, with four 3-pounders on the quarterdeck and a brace of 3-pounder guns on the forecastle. The heavier 28-gun frigate carried 22 9-pounders on the gun deck with six 4-pounders on the upper works. The largest first-generation frigates carried 32 guns – 22 9-pounders on the gun deck, and ten 4-pounder guns on the upper works.

By the start of the American War of Independence the standard frigate had grown, and the 24-gun frigate was becoming obsolete. It was replaced by the more powerful

The gun deck of Constitution. United States *would have had a similar arrangement. Only the captain lived on the gun deck, although his cabins took up much of the ship's stern. (US Navy)*

SHIPS' RATINGS

There is frequent reference to a ship's rating in works on sailing-era naval combat. *Constitution* was rated at "44 guns," and the British frigates in the 1812 frigate duels were all "38-gun" frigates. Yet *Constitution* carried as many as 54 guns, and *Guerrière* 48.

By 1812 a ship's rating was more an administrative tool than a reflection of the number of guns it carried. It set the size of the crew, the officers' pay, and the stores allocated to a ship. Originally, before the introduction of the carronade, it did represent the number of long guns a ship carried. But carronades were so much lighter than long guns that they could be placed where it was impossible or impractical to mount a long gun. The first carronades were added to a ship's battery of great guns, but though ships now carried more guns than their rating suggested, parsimonious admiralties did not raise the ships' ratings because it would have increased costs.

Ratings became more confused when carronades replaced upper deck long guns (or even the main battery). At that point a ship's rating reflected the minimum number of carriage guns it should carry, rather than the actual number.

This administrative fiction is well illustrated by *Chesapeake*, which at launch was rated at 44 guns, even though it was smaller than the 36-gun frigates *Congress* and *Constellation*. Later it was re-rated by the US Navy at 36 guns, and when the British captured it, they rated it a 38-gun frigate.

More confusion was created by differences in the two navies' ratings. The US Navy only had three ratings for frigates: 44-gun, 36-gun, and 32-gun. The Royal Navy's scheme was different, and as it also dominated naval writing in the nineteenth century, it led to American ships being described by their British ratings. *Congress* is often called a 38, and *John Adams* a 28, even though the US Navy rated the ships respectively as 36- and 32-gun frigates.

28-gun frigate, usually mounting 12-pounder guns, although some 9-pounder frigates were still being launched and commissioned. Given the advantages in hitting power, it was obvious that captains would want the heaviest broadside weight of shot that their ships could carry. Yet larger guns were heavier and had greater recoil. To withstand the weight of the guns and the shock of firing them, ships with heavy guns required more substantial structural timbers, or "scantlings." Here we see an additional advantage to the single-deck configuration, for the weight that on two-deckers had been taken up by extra guns could in a frigate be devoted to bigger scantlings, allowing the ship to carry heavier and more usable firepower.

The most dramatic frigate development occurred during the American Revolution, driven primarily by France and the Revolutionary American States. The French started building frigates of unprecedented sizes, with gun decks over 140ft long. The newly independent United States followed, building two frigates with gun decks over 150ft long, and the new US Navy equipped one of their ships with a battery of 18-pounder guns, a caliber previously associated with ships of the line. The British imitated their enemies' practice. By the end of the war, the standard frigate being built by all nations was between 140ft and 150ft long, and armed with 18-pounder long guns on the main deck.

Another radical innovation that occurred during the American Revolution was the introduction of the carronade, a short-barreled, short-range gun designed by the Carron Company of Scotland, which took advantage of the new metallurgy technology of the late eighteenth century. The barrels of carronades were much shorter than those of long guns, but were bored for a much larger ball. Carronades also had less windage than long guns. Windage was the difference between the size of the ball and the bore of the gun. Greater windage – having the ball smaller than the bore – allowed balls to be more easily loaded into the gun without getting stuck. However, it also allowed expanding gas to escape around the sides of the ball, reducing the power of the shot.

Because carronades were bored more precisely than traditional long guns, a smaller charge could be used, allowing a lighter gun. Carronades could therefore be mounted on decks too light to mount heavy cannon. Larger carronades, especially the 24-pounder and 32-pounder carronades, were also more effective than the 4-pounder or 6-pounder upper work long guns they replaced. They had the same effective range as the light long guns, but a lot more hitting power at close ranges.

During the American Revolution only the Royal Navy had carronades, but by the start of the French Revolutionary Wars in 1793 other navies were adopting them. By 1812, all navies were using them, and none more so than the Royal Navy and the US Navy. By 1812, most sloops, brigs and other small, single-deck warships in both navies were armed almost exclusively with carronades, except for a pair of long chase guns in the bows. While all but the most elderly frigates retained a main battery of long guns, the guns on the upper works were almost exclusively carronades. US Navy frigates generally carried a pair of long guns on the forecastle, while the Royal Navy often carried four long guns on the upper works – two in the forecastle, and two as the aftermost guns on the quarterdeck.

THE ROYAL NAVY FRIGATE

By the War of 1812 the Royal Navy had been superintending the design of frigates for well over half a century. Early British frigate designs had had problems, and throughout the eighteenth century they were notorious for being too small, too weakly armed and possessing poor sailing qualities. The Royal Navy eliminated these design problems through a decade of intense effort in the 1790s, and by the time hostilities with France resumed, following the Peace of Amiens, British frigate designs were superior to those of any other European nation.

The first radical step was actually taken in the 1780s, when the Royal Navy ceased designing frigates to carry a 12-pounder or 9-pounder main battery. Except for a few unsuccessful experiments, all frigates designed after 1783 were intended to carry 18-pounder long guns on their main decks, and had scantlings sturdy enough to accept the weight and recoil of these big guns. Most French frigates equipped for sea service were given a 12-pounder battery, in order not to overstress the more lightly built French frigates. This often included the frigates the French were building that were capable of carrying 18-pounder guns.

The French had experimented with frigates designed to carry a 24-pounder main battery in the years prior to the French Revolution, which culminated in the 40-gun frigates of the *Pomone* class. The French also converted obsolete 64-gun ships of the line into frigates by removing the upper works and converting the upper gun deck into a quarterdeck and forecastle. This process was called "razeeing" (for razor) and the ships so converted were called razees.

The British briefly emulated these French trends in the 1790s. After capturing *Pomone* in 1794, they built a frigate that copied its lines, but which was constructed with heavier British scantlings. The result, the 40-gun *Endymion*, proved a popular command. At the same time, they also converted three 64-gun ships of the line into 44-gun razees, including the ship that would become Sir Edward Pellew's famous *Indefatigable*. They too, were successful and popular.

The extra firepower of the 24-pounder frigate proved unnecessary and uneconomical. Standard British frigate designs carrying 18-pounder batteries easily triumphed over French and Spanish 24-pounder frigates, and the 24-pounder frigate required extra men to handle the heavier guns. Lacking utility, the British relegated the 24-pounder frigate to history by 1800. *Endymion*, when in commission between 1800 and 1812, was only equipped with 18-pounder guns.

Having decided on its optimal main weapon for its frigates, Britain focused on perfecting its 18-pounder frigate designs. By the resumption of the war with France in 1803, the Admiralty had settled into a few basic frigate designs that were used for most subsequent construction, the most important of which were the 36-gun *Apollo* class, and the 38-gun *Leda* and *Lively* classes. Most of the frigates ordered between 1803 and 1812 belonged to one of these three classes.

These designs had much in common. The keels of all of these frigate designs ranged between 121ft and 125ft, yielding a gun deck of 145ft (the *Apollo*s) to 155ft (the

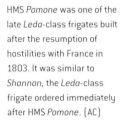

HMS *Undaunted* belonged to the *Lively* class, one of two major classes of 38-gun frigates built for the Royal Navy in the Napoleonic era. It is shown here as it appeared in the 1820s. (AC)

HMS *Pomone* was one of the late *Leda*-class frigates built after the resumption of hostilities with France in 1803. It was similar to *Shannon*, the *Leda*-class frigate ordered immediately after HMS *Pomone*. (AC)

*Lively*s) in length. The average gun deck of the *Leda*-class frigates was 151ft. The length of the larger two classes allowed their main deck battery to mount one extra gun per side: they carried 14 18-pounders on each broadside, while the *Apollo*s had only 13. All three designs were excellent sailers, and had outstanding sea-keeping characteristics. The 38-gun classes were a distillation of the best of British and French naval architecture.

The *Leda* was a derivative of a French design. Its lines were taken from the *Hebe*, a 40-gun 18-pounder frigate captured from the French in 1782. The British modified the design slightly, and also built it with heavier scantlings, consistent with their typical practice. (Britain had better access to shipbuilding timber than France throughout the period. As a result, the French were often forced to skimp on materials.) However, the *Leda*s had problems with space and storage. They had finer hull lines and a shallower hold than earlier British frigate designs, and, as a result, the captains of these frigates had difficulty stowing the regulation amount of stores.

Those problems were addressed in the *Lively* class. These ships were longer, with fuller hulls and deeper holds than the *Leda*s. In many ways they represented the ultimate development of the 38-gun, 18-pounder frigate. The *Lively* class was preferred by the Navy Board and by frigate captains, but the *Leda*s remained more popular with the Admiralty, and remained in production longer.

The French also used *Hebe* as the basis for their subsequent classes of heavy frigates built between 1789 and 1806. As a result, when the British captured these ships, they found themselves with a near sister of their own standard frigates. Thus, prize frigates, including *Guerrière*, could be added to the British fleet with little modification.

It should be stressed that the British used the 38-gun frigate as their standard because it best suited the needs of the Royal Navy during the period from 1803 to 1812. It was not because the Royal Navy was incapable of building larger frigates – indeed, the Royal Navy had several excellent designs for 24-pounder frigates that dated back to the 1790s. Once the first frigate duels in the War of 1812 revealed that the standard design was inadequate to defeat an American 24-pounder frigate, the Royal Navy reacted promptly, embarking on an emergency program to build their own super-frigates. Several were built using the lines of *Endymion*, while others, including the 50-gun *Leander* class of frigates, were new designs. To speed construction, the Royal Navy built these ships out of pitch pine. This may have created the misconception in the British press that the American 44s were also built of fir. The Royal Navy also razeed three small 74-gun ships of the line, to create super-frigates with a 32-pounder main battery.

THE US NAVY FRIGATE

Frigate design in the United States followed a different path to that of Britain. The challenges faced by both nations were different, so each nation came up with a design tailored to its needs. In the case of the Royal Navy, the challenge was to build and man enough ships to maintain mastery of the seas, and protect widely scattered interests. The United States, on the other hand, was faced with the need for an ability to project focused power to protect American interests. The biggest problem its navy faced was the relative poverty of the Federal Government. While the United States was resource-rich, in the first three decades of its existence it was cash-poor. The cost and the power of the Federal Government were kept to a minimum.

As a result the emphasis was on economical warships – ships offering the best balance of firepower and speed at the lowest possible cost. Ships of the line were viewed as too slow and too expensive – both in terms of manpower and money – for the American budget. Instead, the navy wanted frigates, which were fast, sufficiently powerful for the United States' needs, and which could be built relatively quickly. As the United States did not expect to ever build and commission enough ships to match

HMS *GUERRIERE*

Length of gun deck: 155ft 9in
Length of keel: 129ft 11½ in
Extreme breadth: 39ft 9in
Depth of hold: 12ft 10in
Displacement: 1,092 tons
Armament at battle: 30 18-pounder long guns, two long 12-pounder long guns (bow chasers), 16 32-pounder carronades, Total weight of broadside: 538lb
Launched: Cherbourg, 1799

Crew: 300 at full complement
Present at battle: 272

Guerrière was one of the numerous prize frigates serving in the Royal Navy in the Napoleonic era. Roughly one-third of the frigates used by the Royal Navy had been captured from other navies. *Guerrière*, like most other prizes, had been taken from the French Navy.

British writers, especially William James, often excuse *Guerrière*'s poor performance in its battle with *Constitution* on the grounds of its age. Yet *Guerrière* was younger than *Constitution*. It would be more accurate to say that *Guerrière* was in poorer repair than *Constitution,* for a number of reasons. First, *Guerrière* was French-built. The French tended to use lighter scantlings than the British, owing to French difficulties in securing ship timber, and ships with lighter scantlings wore out more quickly. *Guerrière* had also seen hard service. The Royal Navy captured it after a 45-minute battle that left 16 percent of the French crew killed or wounded, and caused the ship significant damage to its hull and masts. After a brief refit, *Guerrière* was recommissioned under British colors, and remained at sea for virtually all of the rest of its life. At the time of its battle with *Constitution* it was overdue for a refit.

those of a major European navy, the emphasis was placed on quality. The US Navy would build only a few frigates, but these were to be the best in the world, capable of beating any other frigate in a single-ship action.

The United States was no novice at shipbuilding, and indeed, it had almost as much experience designing and building frigates as the Royal Navy. Its shipyards had been building large warships – including frigates and two-deckers – since the mid-eighteenth century. During the American Revolution, the colonies had built more than a dozen frigates, several of which were revolutionary designs. The *Warren* was one of the first frigates to carry 18-pounder guns, and, with gun decks in excess of 150ft in length, *Alliance* and *Confederacy* were also unusually large frigates for their time.

When the United States decided to build a navy in 1794, it not only decided to build six frigates, it decided to build the most powerful frigates in the world. In the words of Joshua Humphreys, the man chosen to design them, they would be "… such frigates as in blowing weather to be an overmatch for common double-deck ships, and in light winds to evade coming to action."

The design Humphreys produced was unprecedented. While other nations had built frigates intended to carry 24-pounders, none had been as large. Humphreys' 44-gun frigate design had a 150ft keel, with a gun deck 175ft in length. This was larger than many ships of the line, and represented the maximum possible for a frigate built exclusively from wood. While longer sailing frigates would be built in the nineteenth century, these ships' wooden timbers were reinforced with iron structural members.

As in other wooden ships with transverse framing, a frigate relied on the strength of its keel – and, to a lesser extent, its continuous decks – for much of its longitudinal strength, as transverse framing resisted longitudinal loads poorly. As the length of ships increased, they became more vulnerable to longitudinal stresses; flexing in the middle as the force of the waves pushed the bow and stern up and down. Fitted with

After numerous US Navy victories, American printmakers mocked the Royal Navy in cartoons. Here, John Bull is seen getting a bloody nose from the American "Brother Jonathan." "Uncle Sam" did not yet exist, emerging as a national personification after the War of 1812. (LOC)

USS *Constitution* was the most famous of the 24-pounder frigates designed by Joshua Humphreys. It is shown here, in Boston Harbor, shortly after the War of 1812. (LOC)

their extra forecastle and quarterdeck guns, a frigate's bow and stern bore the greatest concentration of the ship's weight; but these were also the narrowest parts of the hull and provided the least amount of buoyancy. As a result, many frigates became "hogged": the keel bending as the ends of the ship sank and the waist was pushed up, leaving the ship dangerously weakened.

Humphreys overcame this problem with three separate solutions. Firstly, he used scantlings of unprecedented thickness. He also linked the quarterdeck and forecastle into one continuous deck, called a spar deck. While the waist of the spar deck was incapable of bearing guns, even carronades, it was significantly stronger than the gangways across the waists of earlier frigates, and these thick timbers provided extra rigidity. Finally, Humphreys built diagonal riders into the sides of his frigates, so reducing the flexing inherent in simple longitudinal planking. As a result, the Humphreys 44s had remarkably durable hulls. The two that survived the War of 1812 were still structurally sound 50 years later, during the American Civil War.

However, because of their size, these were controversial designs. They required masts and spars that were much larger than was traditional for a frigate in order to get their best turn of speed. When first commissioned, they were too lightly sparred and sailed poorly. As a result of these frigates' performance during the Quasi-War with France (1798–1800), as well as the abandoning of the 24-pounder frigate by European navies, the United States also abandoned the concept. It changed the plans for the fourth 44-gun frigate authorized, and although kept on the books as a "44-gun frigate," it had a shorter hull with scantlings for an 18-pounder main battery.

The result, *Chesapeake*, was a frigate no larger than the British *Leda*s and *Lively*s. It, along with a follow-on design, *Philadelphia*, were rated as 44-gun frigates until

1811, when *Chesapeake* was re-rated at 36 guns. This was more of an acknowledgment of reality than a change in policy. *Chesapeake* was actually smaller than the two 36-gun frigates designed by Humphreys in 1794.

In addition to the six frigates authorized in 1794, the United States built seven other frigates at the start of the Quasi-War. Two were built to carry an 18-pounder main battery: *Philadelphia*, designated a 44-gun frigate, and *New York*, rated 36 guns, and a near sister to Humphreys' other 36-gun designs. The other six frigates, rated at 32 guns, were anachronisms. In the age of heavy frigates, these were both too small and too weak, only capable of carrying 12-pounder long guns on their main deck. These smaller frigates wore out quickly, in part owing to the American habit of cramming the heaviest possible battery into its warships. By the War of 1812 all had been rebuilt at least once, and one, *Constellation*, was undergoing a second major rebuild in a little over a decade of use.

Only one, *Essex*, sailed as a frigate during the War of 1812, but it was rearmed with a main battery of carronades – armament appropriate to a sloop of war. The remainder were rebuilt as sloops of war, used as cartel ships, or kept in port. At the outbreak of war, the US Navy's main punch lay with Humphreys' three 44-gun frigates, the 24-pounder design that was then believed a design dead end.

The difference in size between the British and United States frigates that participated in the four frigate duels of the War of 1812 are shown below. As can be seen, the American ships are larger than both the British and French designs. The Humphreys design displaced 45 percent more than a British 38-gun frigate. Even *Chesapeake*, cramped by American standards, had 15 percent more capacity than its British counterpart.

Physical Dimension of Frigates				
Ship	Length of gun deck (feet)	Extreme breadth (feet)	Depth of hold (feet)	Tonnage (tons)
US Navy				
Constitution, United States	175	46.5	23.5	1,576
Chesapeake	152.5	40	14	1,244
Royal Navy				
Guerrière	155.75	39.75	12.83	1,092
Macedonian	154.5	39.5	13.6	1,081
Java	152.5	40	12.75	1,073
Shannon	150.17	40	12.92	1,066

USS *CONSTITUTION*

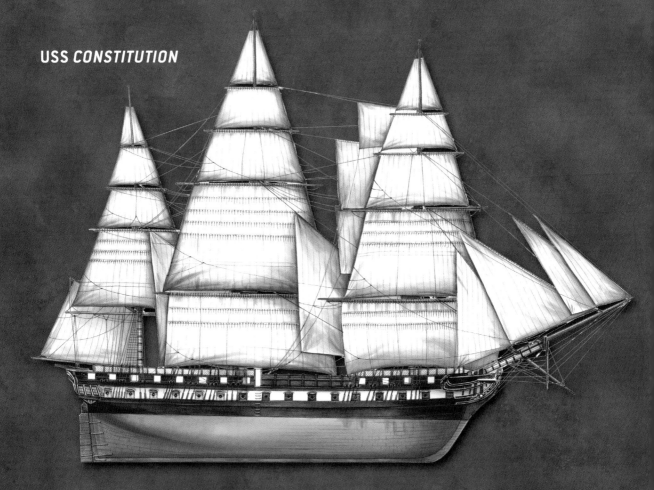

Length of gun deck: 175ft
Length of keel: 150ft
Extreme breadth: 46ft 6in
Depth of hold: 23ft 6in
Displacement: 1576 tons
Armament at battle: 32 24-pounder long guns (two replacing original 18-pounder long guns on spar deck as bow chasers), 22 32-pounder carronades
Total weight of broadside: 704lb
Launched: October 21, 1797

Crew: 475 at full complement
Present at battle: 456

Constitution had several advantages over *Guerrière*. *Constitution* was nearly 50 percent larger and was built significantly stronger. Joshua Humphreys specified scantlings that were much heavier than those traditionally used on frigates. The hull was further strengthened by live oak construction and diagonal riders.

Live oak was unique to the United States. Live oak is 50 percent stronger than white oak (as used by the British), and so lasted 12 years rather than eight. *Constitution* was also one of the earliest ships to be built with diagonal riders – thick structural timbers placed diagonally to the frames and keel. Riders reduced a hull's tendency to hog (sink at the ends) or sag (sink in the middle).

The result was an extremely strong hull, well equipped to resist the stresses of both hard sailing and battle damage, especially that caused by the 18-pounder long guns and low-velocity carronades mounted by British standard frigates. It is easy to see why the Royal Navy must have felt that *Constitution* indeed had "iron sides."

THE STRATEGIC SITUATION

The War of 1812 was a war that both sides blundered into, rather than one started with any deliberate intent. Since 1793, Britain had been locked in a global war with France, its great Continental rival. From 1805 through 1811, despite a naval victory at Trafalgar that gave it command of the seas, Britain believed that it was losing. With its energy focused on the war with Napoleon, it had no interest in seeking another with its former colonies. But the United States, newly independent and an ocean away from the main battlefields of the Napoleonic Wars, objected both to British restrictions on America's trade with Europe and to the Royal Navy's custom of "impressing" – forcibly drafting – American sailors into their service.

Following Broke's capture of *Chesapeake,* British cartoonists returned the compliment. Here, sturdy British tars are shown beating cowardly Americans. (LOC)

BRITISH VALOUR and YANKEE BOASTING or, Shannon versus Chesapeake.

In 1806, France and Britain had begun waging economic warfare upon one another. France's Berlin Decrees of 1806 were intended to paralyze Britain's trade by prohibiting its allies and neutrals from trading with Britain. Britain retaliated with their first Orders in Council in 1807, which in turn restricted the right of neutrals to trade with France.

Prohibited from trading with Europe by the combined legislation of the two warring sides, the United States countered with the Embargo Act, which closed American ports to international commerce. The Act threw the United States into a recession, but failed to harm either European rival. The Embargo Act was repealed in 1808, but not before it forced unemployed American sailors to seek work overseas, including in the Royal Navy and British merchant ships (from which they were often pressed into the Royal Navy). Meanwhile Britain enacted more restrictive Orders in Council in 1809, further tightening the United States' trade with Europe.

Equally onerous to the United States was the custom of impressment. The Royal Navy's fleets needed skilled manpower, and after 15 years of almost continuous warfare it was desperate for men. Britain historically had manned its ships during wartime through the conscription of British and colonial merchant sailors. But many Americans had been born in Britain, and others had accents virtually indistinguishable from those of British colonies like Nova Scotia, Bermuda, or the Caribbean islands. Others born in the United States had voluntarily or involuntarily served in the Royal Navy, with tattoos marking their British service. Royal Navy officers seeking hands often ignored a sailor's claims of American citizenship, either being unable or unwilling to differentiate between real and faux Americans. The United States, as a matter of sovereignty, felt it had to protect the rights of its citizens.

By 1811, the United States Congress felt that threatening war was the only way to seek redress from Britain on these issues. At stake was the pride the United States felt in its own self-determination. An extra temptation was the opportunity it would have to march north and seize Canada. The simmering tensions over impressment had been exacerbated by two notorious naval clashes. In 1807, the 50-gun *Leopard* had fired into the American frigate *Chesapeake*, boarded it, and seized three sailors; and in 1811, while seeking HMS *Guerrière* to recover an impressed American citizen, USS *President* found and fired into the sloop of war HMS *Little Belt*, killing ten. In 1812, the United States delivered its demands as an ultimatum. Britain did not want to be distracted from the European struggle by war with America, and it lifted its Orders in Council on June 16, 1812 and offered compromises on impressment. Congress, unaware of these offers, declared war on June 18.

The War of 1812 appeared to be a strategic mismatch, with the US Navy in a hopeless position. In January 1812, the Royal Navy was the world's most powerful maritime force, with 102 ships of the line, 124 frigates, and 76 ship-rigged sloops of war in commission. It also had 144 brigs of war, 54 cutters, and 37 support vessels in commission. It had 108,600 sailors and 31,400 marines to man these vessels. For command, it could draw upon a pool of 126 admirals, 745 captains and commanders, and 3,730 lieutenants and masters, if superannuated officers were ignored.

The US Navy, in contrast, had no ships of the line, just 11 frigates, three sloops of war, and six brigs of war. Only five of the frigates were ready for sea when war was declared. Of the frigates laid up in reserve, only three were capable of going to sea – one of them only after conversion to a sloop of war. At the start of the war, the US Navy could boast only 5,230 sailors and 1,523 marines, including those who served onshore and on the inland lakes. By war's end, the US Navy, including officers, would grow to 14,960 sailors and 2,715 marines. The officer corps consisted of just 12 captains, ten masters commandant (commanders), 73 lieutenants and 53 masters. The Royal Navy still had more admirals than the US Navy had commissioned officers.

But as American naval officers realized, things were not quite as hopeless as they appeared on paper. In 1812 the Royal Navy was involved in a global war against France and its allies, and few of its 680 warships were stationed in the quiet waters of North America. In these waters, the Royal Navy had only three ships of the line and one 50-gun two-decker. These ships were all elderly or small, and served as flagships for the four squadrons the British had in North America. The Royal Navy's Leeward Station covered the Eastern Caribbean; Jamaica Station was responsible for the Gulf of Mexico and Western Caribbean; North America Station, headquartered in Halifax, was responsible for the United States coast and the middle latitudes of the North Atlantic; and Newfoundland Station covered Canadian waters and the northern North Atlantic.

In addition to the flagship, the Leeward had three frigates and 11 sloops of war; Jamaica Station had four frigates and 11 sloops of war, and Newfoundland Station three frigates and five sloops of war. The North America squadron, which most directly faced the US Navy, had five frigates, including three 38-gun frigates, and 11 sloops. In addition, the four British commands had a further 24 smaller warships. These were too small to fight frigates, but served as dispatch vessels and as convoy escorts.

But even this meager Royal Navy force could not dedicate itself solely to fighting the US Navy. They also had to protect British mercantile shipping across the northwest Atlantic from French warships and privateers, and from outright pirates seeking to take

James Dacres was a typical Royal Navy frigate captain of 1812. Competent but unimaginative, he belonged to the school that preferred trading yardarm-to-yardarm broadsides over maneuvering. (AC)

advantage of the opportunities war offered. They also had to counter the numerous American privateers commissioned since the start of the War of 1812. While the Royal Navy had 80 warships and nearly 12,000 men in American waters opposing only 14 US Navy warships and perhaps 4,000 men, they also had to cover a lot of ocean.

The Americans had another advantage when the war began. North America, and even the Caribbean, was regarded by the British as a backwater. While the Royal Navy had some good and even excellent officers in North America, such as Philip Broke, the vast majority of the rising stars were assigned to more active theaters. Even with the increasing tensions in 1810 and 1811, most British captains in American waters were pedestrian commanders. Many were too well connected to be denied a command, but a posting to North America was meant to keep such commanders out of harm's way.

An additional advantage, unknown to the Americans, was that the British were initially unwilling to press home an attack on American shores. The British view was that war with America was an undesired distraction, and that it had started over a misunderstanding. Initially the British government reasoned that the United States would repeal the declaration of war as soon as Congress learned that the Orders in Council, one of the major *casus belli*, had been rescinded.

It was wishful thinking, ignoring the continuing American anger over impressment, and the lure of adding Canada to the United States. But for the first year of the war, the commander of the Royal Navy's North America Station, Vice-Admiral Herbert Sawyer, attempted to limit the war to a naval one, neither blockading American ports nor raiding American shores. Once the British decided to focus their attention on North America, or the European war ended – as it did in 1814 – the Royal Navy could bring its entire weight down on the fledgling American navy and crush it. But in 1812, this window of opportunity allowed the US Navy to go on the offensive.

Yet not everything favored the United States. While individual US Navy ships were equal to or larger than their British counterparts – apart from the two small subscription frigates *Essex* and *John Adams* – there were few of them. The odds favored them in single-ship actions, but it required luck to find a lone British frigate, given

In the war's opening weeks, both sides had a lone frigate harried by an enemy squadron. HMS *Belvidera* escaped from Rodgers' squadron of three frigates and a sloop of war. In July, in company with *Africa, Shannon, Guerrière,* and *Aeolus, Belvidera* returned the favor, pursuing and nearly capturing *Constitution.* (LOC)

BATTLES
① *Constitution* vs *Guerrière* ④ *Chesapeake* vs *Shannon*
② *United States* vs *Macedonian* ⑤ *Hornet* vs *Peacock*
③ *Constitution* vs *Java*

MAJOR BRITISH STATIONS IN NORTH AMERICA
Ⓐ *Halifax* Ⓒ *Leeward Islands*
Ⓑ *Newfoundland* Ⓓ *Jamaica*

UNITED STATES NAVAL YARDS
Ⓐ *Washington* Ⓔ *Baltimore*
Ⓑ *Boston* Ⓕ *Norfolk*
Ⓒ *Philadelphia* Ⓖ *New Orleans*
Ⓓ *New York*

the vast range the Royal Navy had to cover. The US Navy was ready to seize fortune while they could. But fortune is a fickle mistress, as its officers knew.

The US Navy wanted to try its steel against the Royal Navy, and the captains of the Royal Navy, with the confidence of a virtually unbroken string of single-ship victories since 1793, were more than willing to accommodate them. The responsibilities of the Royal Navy forced their frigates to cruise alone. The inclinations of the American captains led them to find excuses to leave the small American squadrons, and seek individual actions. The result – at least from June 1812 through June 1813 – was an environment highly conducive to single-ship duels.

TECHNICAL SPECIFICATIONS

ARMAMENT

The American 44-gun frigates *Constitution*, *United States*, and *President* carried a main armament of 24-pounder long guns – 15 on each side of the gun deck and two in the bows, on the spar deck, as chase guns. Of these, 18 were 10½ft long and 12 were 9½ft long. Loaded with an 8lb charge of gunpowder and fired at an 11-degree elevation, these extremely powerful guns could fire a 24lb iron ball more than 2,800 yards. With that charge, their point-blank range was nearly 300 yards. These guns weighed between 5,200lb and 5,300lb.

Charged with 4lb of powder, a 6½ft short 24-pounder (mostly used in the upper decks of two-deckers and ships of the line) would penetrate 62in of oak, with enough force to disable a gun carriage mounted behind the wood. The Humphreys frigates' long 24-pounders could penetrate proportionally more, perhaps 90in.

The British 38-gun frigates that fought single-ship actions with American frigates during the War of 1812 were armed with 18-pounder long guns. As with the 24-pounder guns, these 18-pounder guns had barrels that were between 9½ft and 10½ft long, but the 18-pounder weighed 1,000lb less. Yet it had nearly the same range as a 24-pounder when both were loaded with a maximum charge, both in terms of maximum and point-blank ranges. However, the maximum charge of an 18-pounder long gun was smaller; 6lb of gunpowder to the 8lb used by the 24-pounders. With a lighter shot propelled by less

OPPOSITE

Carronades actually threw shot more accurately than long guns, because carronades had less windage. However, when the standard practice of aiming along the top of the barrel was followed, the tapered carronade barrel meant its ball would accurately fly over the target. The variety of carronades illustrated here are those used by the Royal Navy. (AC)

powder, an 18-pounder long gun had only half the hitting power of a 24-pounder gun, and was capable of penetrating only 42in of oak. Armed with such guns, the British frigates facing the Humphreys 44-gun frigates were at a distinct disadvantage.

Nor did the British gain any advantage when the guns on the upper works were considered. *Constitution* and *Chesapeake* carried 32-pounder carronades during their single-ship actions. *United States* and *President* were armed with 42-pounder carronades. The British frigates carried 32-pounder carronades on their upper works, as well as either a pair of 12-pounder or two or four 9-pounder long guns as chase weapons.

The barrel of a 32-pounder carronade weighed around 2,000lb, less than half the weight of a long 18-pounder, and just a few hundred pounds more than the 6-pounder long gun it replaced on the upper works. A 32-pounder carronade charged with 2lb 10oz of gunpowder had a range of 1,090 yards when fired at a 5-degree elevation. Point-blank range with that charge was 330 yards – longer than that of the long guns carried by these frigates. The huge 42-pounder carronade weighed little more, at 2,500lb. With its standard charge of 3½lb of gunpowder, it could throw a 42lb ball 1,170 yards when fired at a 5-degree elevation. It had a point-blank range of 400 yards.

Most naval battles were fought at musket shot (100 yards) or pistol shot (30 yards) range, and carronades should have been highly accurate at these ranges. But one aspect of a carronade caused its very accuracy to work against it. Sights were rarely fitted to naval guns in the eighteenth century, and gunners aimed by sighting along the top of the barrel. As the breech end of the carronade was significantly wider than the muzzle end, a carronade aimed in that manner would be fired about three degrees above the target. Long guns had a pronounced muzzle swell, which reduced this tendency to shoot high. In fact, a manually-sighted long gun naturally aimed only about half a degree higher than the aiming point – an error that over short ranges almost exactly compensated for the fall of shot caused by gravity.

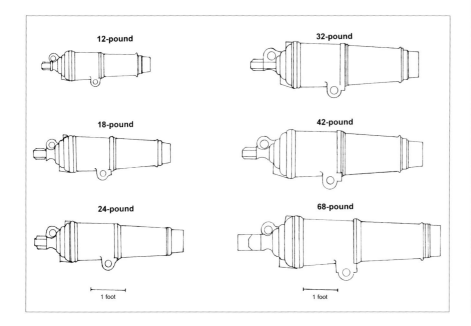

12-pound

18-pound

24-pound

32-pound

42-pound

68-pound

1 foot

1 foot

The most devastating blow that could be landed on a ship was a stern rake. The stern of the ship, squared-off and filled with windows, offered no resistance to a shot hitting it. The ball would fly down the length of the ship, cutting down anyone and anything in its path. This shows *Constitution* raking *Java*. This broadside sheared off *Java*'s mainmast at the top. (FDRL)

Live-fire target practice was rare during the eighteenth century, and virtually all practice firing was done with the chase guns, which were long guns. Often, the only time a ship's crew aimed at a target with all of its guns was in combat. As a result, crews did not get the chance to adjust to the carronade, and carronades gained an unfair reputation for being inaccurate at any but the shortest ranges – the ranges at which firing high did not matter.

This error could be corrected by fitting dispart sights to carronades, which allowed the gunner to sight the gun true to its bore. By the start of the nineteenth century good frigate captains, both British and American, were fitting their carronades with dispart sights and conducting live target practice with their carronades. Often, captains paid for the sights and the practice powder and shot out of their own pocket.

At the time of its battle with *Guerrière*, *Constitution* carried 22 32-pounder carronades, and 20 when it fought *Java*. *Guerrière* and *Java* carried 16 and 18 32-pounder carronades respectively on their quarterdecks and forecastle. *United States* had 22 42-pounder carronades to *Macedonian*'s 16 32-pounders. *Chesapeake* had 18 32-pounder carronades while *Shannon* mounted 16 32-pounders.

STRUCTURE

The ability to absorb punishment was as relevant to a ship's chance of victory as its ability to wreak damage. This was a function of both a ship's size and its construction. Again, the American frigates had the edge in this respect. The table on page 21 gives the principal dimensions of the seven frigates involved in the four

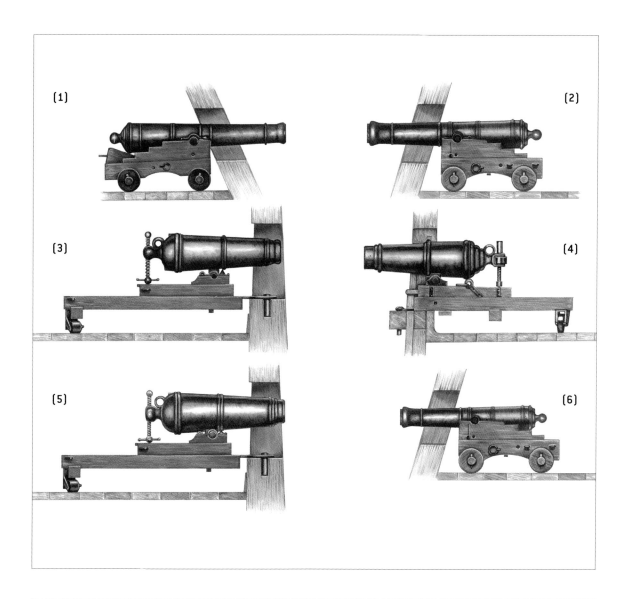

(1)   (2)   (3)   (4)   (5)   (6)

GREAT GUNS

By the War of 1812, both navies had standardized their arsenals around a specific set of guns. For the US Navy, the main battery gun of choice was (1) the 24-pounder long gun. Many were purchased from the Royal Navy in 1798–99, and were still in service in 1812. Over half of the *Constitution*'s 24-pounders were British. The Royal Navy opted for (2) the 18-pounder long gun, 20 percent lighter than the 24-pounder, but with a ball 75 percent of the weight of the larger gun.

For the upper deck, both sides preferred large carronades. The American frigates mounted either (3) 32-pounder carronades or (5) the larger 42-pounder carronades. The three 44-gun frigates normally mounted 42-pounder carronades, with the lighter frigates carrying 32-pounder carronades. At the start of the War of 1812 *Constitution* had a spar deck battery of 32-pounder carronades, but these were replaced with 42-pounders after its battle with *Java*.

Royal Navy frigates carried (4) 32-pounder carronades on their upper works. Additionally, most British frigates carried (6) the highly accurate 9-pounder long gun as chase guns. Normally four were carried, with one pair in the bow and one in the stern. James Dacres of *Guerrière*, however, replaced his 9-pounder bow chasers with 12-pounders.

frigate duels of the War of 1812. The American 44-gun frigates were nearly 50 percent larger than their British counterparts, and even *Chesapeake* displaced 17 percent more than *Shannon*.

But more important to a ship's ability to absorb damage was the strength of its hull structure. Here, too, the Humphreys 44-gun frigates had a decisive edge. In order to bear the weight and recoil of the 24-pounder main battery, Humphreys had specified unprecedently thick scantlings. The keel and keelson were each 18in thick, and the frames ranged from 15in wide at the gun deck to 2ft at the keel. Additionally, the main framing of the ship was made from live oak, a tree unique to the southern United States. It was 50 percent stronger than white oak, as used by British shipwrights.

Chesapeake, while smaller than the Humphreys frigates, was also built from live oak, and it too had oversized scantlings. Originally intended as a fourth Humphreys frigate, it was redesigned to smaller European dimensions prior to construction, but only once timber for its construction had already been assembled. The timbers used to build her had therefore been scaled for a larger ship.

The keel of a British 38-gun frigate would have been approximately 15½in wide, with corresponding frames 11in to 13in thick. British-built frigates were typically built using white oak for the structure, although if ships were needed quickly, red oak or various pines were substituted. While both *Macedonian* and *Shannon* were wartime constructions, both were built from white oak, perhaps the best building material for warships except live oak. Both were soundly made warships, albeit more lightly built than their American counterparts.

The same may not have been true of either *Guerrière* or *Java*. Both were French prizes, and *Java* had been built in 1805, after the resumption of hostilities with Britain. French shipwrights had trouble finding adequate white oak even during peacetime, and as France's domestic timber was usually shipped by sea, the British blockade of the French coast caused significant problems for French shipwrights. Wartime French ships therefore often used inferior wood, and were built with lighter scantlings than their British counterparts. Prize frigates such as *Guerrière* and *Java* would have been significantly weaker than *Shannon* or *Macedonian*.

Firing smoothbore cannon quickly required constant practice just to master the mechanics of running the one- to three-ton pieces in and out. This dumb-show practice may have trained gunners to fire quickly, but actually hitting a target required live-fire practice. (AC)

PROPULSION

In common with ships of the line and large sloops, frigates were full-rigged ships. This meant they had three masts, all of which had square sails, as well as fore-and-aft sails. By 1812, the main driving sails of a ship were the topsails, particularly those on the foremast and mainmast. The courses, set on the lower masts, and the topgallants, rigged on removable masts immediately above the topsails, were used for fast cruising. Masts were broken into three or four sections, each of which was progressively slimmer, and set into a step at the top of the mast below. The lower masts were set onto the keel of the ship.

On most frigates of that period, a royal yard and sail could be set on the topgallant mast, above the topgallant sail. Sails set above the first sail on a mast segment – and therefore without their own mast – were said to be set "flying." On the biggest frigates, which included the American 44s, a royal mast would be rigged above the topgallant, and the royal sail set on that.

The sails on the aft (or mizzen) mast contributed relatively little to a frigate's speed, and nor did the sails above the topgallants – royals, skysails, and moonsails. Along with the studdingsails – fair-weather sails rigged outboard of the square sails on yardarm extensions – these small sails added a few knots to a ship's speed, but were used only for cruising in light winds.

Indeed, you could actually slow a sailing ship by setting too much canvas, especially on the upper masts. As wind pushes on a sail, the mast acts as a lever on the hull, heeling the ship to leeward. The higher above the deck a sail was set, the more heeling

Sail plan of a US Navy frigate, with component sails labeled. This depicts a 24-pounder frigate as it would have appeared in the 1820s. Note the segmentation of the masts into lower mast, topmast and topgallant segments. (AC)

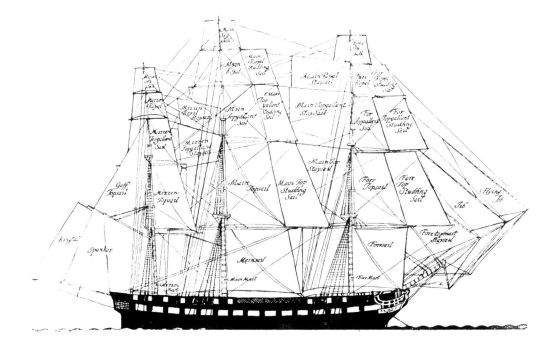

BATTLE SAIL

Most captains switched to "battle sail" (**above**) before trading broadsides, a configuration which gave a ship the speed it needed to fight, while allowing the crew to concentrate on working the guns. The courses (lowest sails) would be "brailed up." Clewlines (at the corners) would be drawn in, and buntlines (in the middle of the sail) pulled up, bunching the courses up near the yard. The topsails – the main driving sails of a frigate – would be set, as well as one of the outer jibs and the spanker in the stern. (These fore-and-aft sails helped steer.) Often, the spanker would be partially pulled in. To add speed, an additional jib could be set, or the courses could be shaken out by releasing the clewlines and buntlines. (**Inset 1**) But this required caution. A set course was low enough that a ship's own guns, when fired, could send burning gunpowder and wadding onto the overhanging sail, risking setting fire to the canvas. To slow, a captain could shorten sail (**Inset 2**). Normally this was done by reefing – folding and tying the upper part of the sail to the spar. Reefing required a lot of men aloft, who in battle would be needed at the great guns. Alternatively, a captain might temporarily dip the topsail yards – lower them without reefing the sail – which effectively reduced the working surface area.

MANEUVERING UNDER SAIL

A frigate's ability to maneuver (**right**) was as much a weapon as its guns, and its sails were used to maneuver as much as for propulsion. The jibs and spanker were used to maneuver by providing leverage at a ship's bow and stern respectively. However, the square sails could also be used, especially through the use of backing the sails.
To back a sail, one pivoted the spar so the wind is blowing the sail back – against the mast. Depending upon which sail was backed, a captain could either stop a ship virtually instantly, or swing a ship's bow or stern around. In the main part of this plate, the mainsail is backed. The ship is hove-to (motionless) as the forward force imparted by the fore and mizzen topsails is balanced by the backward force of the backed main topsail. **Inset 1** shows how backing the fore topsail while keeping the main and mizzen sails filled can be used to push the bow in a particular direction (in this case to the viewer's right or the ship's left). This helps the ship tack – change the direction that the wind is hitting the ship. **Inset 2** shows how backing the mizzen topsail can be used to slew the stern of the ship around, as the hull pivots about the mainmast. Isaac Hull used this maneuver to keep *Constitution*'s broadside bearing on *Guerrière* longer.

1

2

Both taking in a sail completely and reefing a sail (shown here) were all-hands operations. To reef, or shorten a sail, sailors spread on a yardarm would reach down the sail and grab a reef point (lengths of rope, attached to the sail at one end, and fixed in bands across the sail). The sailors would haul the sail up and tie the reef points to the spar (or later a jackstay) all the while being careful not to slip. This was one reason why ships shifted to battle sails before action, as it freed the crew to work on the guns. (AC)

force a specific strength of wind produced. Exacerbating this was the fact that wind speed increases with the height above the water.

Every ship had a heeling angle at which optimum speed was reached. Once heeled beyond that angle, the pressure would force the hull to start slipping to leeward, slightly perpendicular to its direction of travel, and therefore slowing the ship. Setting and trimming the optimal combination of sails for any particular set of conditions was a task requiring outstanding seamanship, gained only through years of practical experience. The fact that their captains had this experience was one reason that sailing navies, such as the US Navy and Royal Navy, could outsail their harbor-bound French and Spanish counterparts, even when the French and Spanish ships had a higher potential speed.

During battle, the upper yards, sails, and masts were frequently lowered, and stowed at the ship's side or in the shrouds. The differences between the mast and sail areas of American and British frigates, while significant, was meaningful only in a pursuit. Since both sides were willing participants in the four single-ship frigate duels, maneuverability was more important than speed.

The three-mast configuration maximized the maneuverability of a full-rigged ship, which pivoted roughly around the mainmast. A captain could use the sails on the mizzenmast to turn the stern of the ship, and those of the foremast to turn the bow. The greatest turning leverage was provided by the fore-and-aft sails – the jibs and staysails ahead of the foremast, and the trapezoidal spanker, or spencer sail behind the mizzenmast. Control of these sails was critical in battle, since the loss of a jib or spanker could cause the ship to slew. Losing the mizzenmast or foremast significantly reduced a frigate's maneuverability. Losing both left a ship unmanageable.

THE COMBATANTS

One of the ironies of the War of 1812 was that the two sets of combatants were so similar. The sailors were recruited from the same pool of people, and the officers of both navies were highly professional and drawn from the same class of society. Conditions and terms of service in both navies were virtually identical.

THE MEN

A frigate was one of the most complicated machines of its day. In addition to its officers, a frigate required a crew of between 200 and 350 men to operate its sails and rigging as well as fight its guns. While there was a role for strong backs and weak minds, a large proportion of sailors needed to be skilled. Additionally, a frigate carried between 25 and 50 marines, to enforce discipline and to provide a ship with a small force of maritime soldiers.

A skilled seaman was able to handle (work the lines controlling the sails), reef (shorten sail), and steer (do a turn at the ship's wheel). In the Royal Navy, such men were rated as able seamen, meriting extra pay. To gain such skills, sailors started their careers early, usually in their early teens or even younger.

Being a sailor was a young man's game. During this era, the vast majority of sailors who worked on the upper masts as "topmen" were in their teens. The captain of the top – an able seaman, who directed the activities on one of the upper masts – was usually a man in his twenties. Older sailors were typically employed on deck, where they did the skilled tasks (such as handling the helm) or supervising the unskilled members of the crew. A frigate generally had plenty of these unskilled "landsmen." As much as possible, these men were employed on deck – handling the gun tackles and hauling on lines handled from the decks – until they gained an ordinary seaman's skills.

But a seaman described as "older" often referred to a man only in his thirties. The "Old Salt" of fiction was a rare creature in the 1810s. Men generally died, became disabled, or moved to warrant ranks or sedentary roles (such as cook) by the time they were in their forties and fifties. Death and disablement were common, and combat was often the smallest risk. Accidents while working aloft or with unforgiving equipment were a frequent cause of injury or death, and disease and shipwreck also took their toll.

A sailor signed a contract to work on a particular ship, rather than signing up with a navy or, in the case of merchantmen, a company. On a merchantman, the contract was for a voyage, and on a warship, it was for the duration of a ship's commission – traditionally three years in peacetime. If a ship were wrecked, the sailors' employment (and pay) ceased.

The allegiance of a warship's crew was therefore typically to the ship, not the nation. Unemployed sailors often signed onto ships belonging to other nations, and even national warships would often have a surprisingly international crew. This was one factor complicating the issue of who exactly was a "British" sailor in the years leading up to the War of 1812. Many American sailors enlisted in ships of the Royal Navy, particularly after the Embargo Act, passed by Congress in 1807, made it difficult to find work on American ships.

There was little difference between the life of a seaman aboard a frigate in the Royal Navy and that of his opposite number in the US Navy. Pay and food was comparable, although food in the smaller United States Navy was frequently of a better quality. Discipline was also similar. Both navies punished trivial offenses with stoppage of privileges, minor offenses with flogging, and major offenses with hanging. Both navies had comparable concepts of what constituted trivial, minor, and major offenses, and certainly, a man was just as likely to be hanged for desertion in both navies.

Both navies also had a number of "flogging captains," who enforced discipline harshly with the tails of the cat. William Bainbridge of the *Constitution* was particularly notorious for this.

The major difference between the two navies lay in their methods of recruitment. Whereas the US Navy was an all-volunteer service in both peace and war, during wartime the Royal Navy used a form of maritime conscription known as impressment. Only mariners were subject to impressment, and only British citizens could be impressed. Traditionally, a sailor was impressed for one commission aboard a

Shipboard routine was regular and regulated. Men stood four- or two-hour watches. Every daybreak in both navies saw the decks being scrubbed down with holystones. (AC)

38

warship, although those with certain critical maritime skills were exempt from impressment. These individuals had a certificate of exemption.

Impressment filled the Royal Navy's temporary need for skilled hands in its expanded wartime fleet, when ships laid up in reserve were recommissioned. It worked well during the eighteenth century, when naval wars were three to five years long, which meant an unwilling sailor usually only served briefly. But the demands of the French Revolutionary and Napoleonic Wars had brought the system close to collapse. By 1812, Britain had been at war, virtually continuously, for nearly two decades. The Royal Navy had expanded to an unprecedented scale, with equally unprecedented manpower requirements.

In 1795, Britain expanded impressment by imposing manpower quotas on local governments, which were often filled by assigning convicts and debtors to the navy. However, even that failed to yield enough manpower, and a pressed sailor would often find himself free once his ship paid off, only to be immediately impressed for another commission. With a seemingly endless war, impressment began appearing to be a life sentence, especially since a sailor's work life was only 20 to 30 years.

Rations Issued to Sailors		
	Royal Navy	**US Navy**
Served daily	1lb bread, ½ pint distilled spirits or 1 pint wine or 1 gallon beer	1lb bread, ½ pint distilled spirits or 1 quart beer
Sunday	2lb pork	1½ lb beef, ½ pint rice
Monday	½ pint peas, 1 pint oatmeal, 2oz butter, 4oz cheese	1lb pork, ½ pint peas or beans, 4oz cheese
Tuesday	2lb beef	1½ lb beef, 1lb turnips, potatoes, or pudding
Wednesday	½ pint peas, 1 pint oatmeal, 2oz butter, 4oz cheese	2oz butter or 6oz molasses, 4oz cheese, ½ pint rice
Thursday	2lb pork, ½ pint peas	1lb pork, ½ pint peas or beans, 4oz cheese
Friday	½ pint peas, 1 pint oatmeal, 2oz butter, 4oz cheese	1lb salt fish, 2oz butter or 1 gill oil, 1lb potatoes
Saturday	2lb beef	1lb pork, ½ pint peas or beans, 4oz cheese

There was little difference between the daily rations issued by both navies, but American sailors enjoyed meat or fish six days each week, while British "tars" had three meatless days each week. The seemingly larger size of the British portions is explained by the existence of the "pursers' measure." In the Royal Navy, a pound of meat was only 14 ounces, and a pound of butter only 12 ounces. While the US Navy issued only a quart of beer daily, sailors in both navies got the same amount of distilled spirits, whether whiskey or rum.

After war resumed in 1803, Britain became less fastidious about limiting impressment to British sailors. The United States and Britain shared a language, and many regional American accents were similar to those found in British territory. Additionally, many Americans were serving on British merchant ships or had previously served on warships.

Other "American" sailors had been born in Britain, and brought to the United States by British parents as infants or children. Although retaining the regional accents of their parents, they thought of themselves as American, not British. Still others emigrated to the United States as adults, seeking the greater opportunities offered by the American frontier, and frequently drifting between the United States and Canada. To confuse matters further, British sailors often claimed American citizenship to gain exemption. Unsurprisingly, British officers often disregarded a sailor's protestations of American citizenship when the officer's ship needed seamen. The result was that by 1812, most British warships had a contingent of Americans serving unwillingly.

A frigate's contingent of marines was deliberately drawn from a different pool than the sailors. In combat most served as marksmen, and were stationed in a ship's fighting tops (the platform where the top of the lower mast met the bottom of the topmast) or along a ship's bulwarks, particularly along the quarterdeck. If the ships came into contact, the marines fought hand-to-hand, either to defend their ship, or take the enemy's vessel. Marines formed the core of boarding parties and any landing parties, if a ship's crew were committed to an action on land.

The marines also provided shipboard security, and were used to maintain discipline. Marine sentries guarded the magazines, arms stores, and spirit room. During battle, marines were posted at the hatches to prevent sailors seeking refuge in the hold. They were also expected to handle lines on deck, and fight a ship's great guns, but they were not used aloft to handle the sails.

Marines were recruited separately from sailors and their training approximated that of soldiers. They slept separately from the sailors, generally between the sailors and a ship's officers. Unlike sailors, marines were issued and wore uniforms. They signed on for a fixed period of time, rather than for a single commission of a ship. Marine contingents were assigned to ships independently of the sailors, and occasionally reassigned to maintain the desired distance from the mariners.

Life aboard a warship was crowded and primitive. The Royal Navy, with its concern over desertion, did not grant shore leave to common seamen. Instead, as shown in this 1812 print, sailors in port entertained themselves aboard ship. Women, ostensibly "wives" were permitted aboard, joining the sailors in raucous amusements and drinking. (LOC)

THE OFFICERS

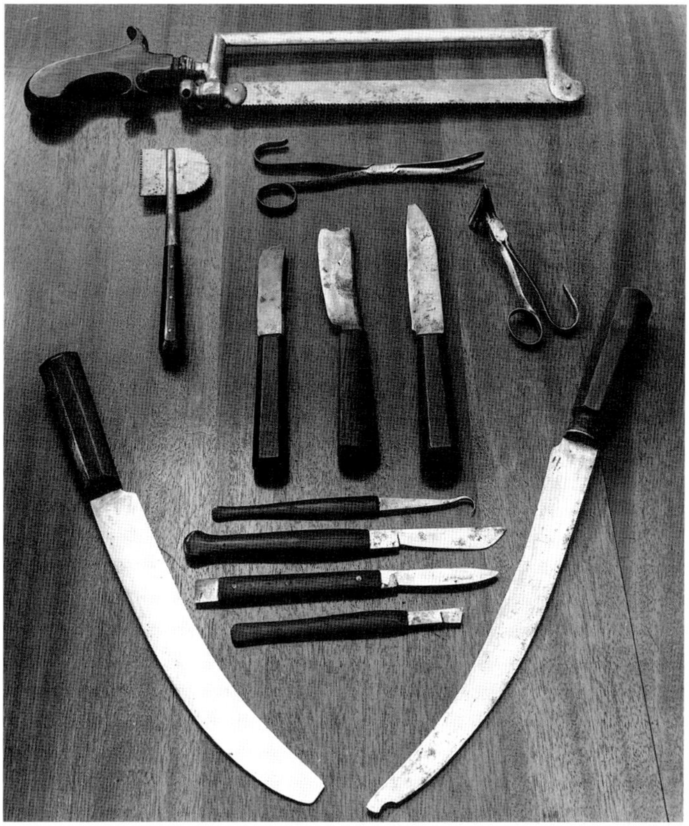

Unlike the men, the officers of both navies identified strongly with their nations. Yet they, too, were similar in training, temperament, and background. Both navies drew their officers primarily from the middle classes. In many ways both navies were meritocracies, allowing a path for intelligent, active men to reach the upper ranks of their nations' society, regardless of origin.

In part, this was due to the demands placed upon a naval officer. Successful commanders required physical bravery, perhaps more than was required from an army officer. In armies, the higher an officer rose, the less exposed to danger he became. Army captains and lieutenants fought alongside their men. Generals directed the battles from behind the lines. Naval captains (the equivalent of army colonels) and admirals not only fought alongside their men, they fought from the most exposed position on a warship – its quarterdeck. The admiral's flagship was often in the thick of the battle, because successful admirals led by example.

A naval officer also needed to navigate his ship, which was a skill requiring mastery of spherical trigonometry, at least on an applied basis. The minimum intelligence for a naval officer was therefore higher than that required for a cavalry officer. Officers were also expected to have mastered the skills possessed by the common seamen they commanded.

Finally, naval service was recognized as a dangerous profession. In addition to the risks of disease and combat, naval officers faced the perils unique to seafarers. Storms, shoals, and unwelcoming coastlines could wreck a ship, killing all aboard. These hazards accounted for nearly three-quarters of the British warships lost during the French Revolutionary and Napoleonic Wars.

Nepotism and influence existed in both navies, but it was always tempered by – at its most basic – the captain's need to sleep. An incompetent watch officer's errors could easily be fatal to all aboard, regardless of the captain's skill. Captains who valued their lives therefore used their influence to promote the most capable individuals to positions of responsibility. A beloved but inept son was better found a position ashore – as a cavalry officer, if the family had the money – than as a naval lieutenant.

A sailor injured in battle received only crude medical care, surgery being performed without anesthesia or antiseptics. The surgeon's tools shown here, consisting of saws, probes, and knives, outlines the period's medical limitations. It was a kit owned by a US Navy surgeon during the War of 1812. (USNHF).

STEPHEN DECATUR

Stephen Decatur was the best-known captain in the US Navy during the War of 1812. He was also quite possibly the best captain in the stellar collection of talent that served America during that war. A man born to the sea, his grandfather had been a mariner; and prior to the American Revolution his father, Stephen Decatur Sr, captained merchant ships. Although the family made its home in Philadelphia, Decatur was born in Maryland's Eastern Shore in 1779, where his mother had fled following the British occupation of Philadelphia. During the Revolution, Decatur Sr served in the Continental Navy. He was later appointed captain in the US Navy after its formation in 1798.

On April 30, 1798, Stephen Decatur secured a midshipman's warrant aboard the *United States*, commanded by his father's friend and Revolutionary War hero John Barry. America was then fighting the Quasi-War with France, and the *United States* spent the war patrolling the Caribbean. Mr Midshipman Decatur was promoted to lieutenant on May 21, 1799, and soon established his reputation for courage and concern for his sailors. When a seaman fell overboard, Decatur plunged into the sea after the man, keeping him afloat until a boat was lowered.

After the Quasi-War, Decatur served in the Mediterranean during America's struggles with the Barbary States: as first lieutenant of *Essex* in 1801–02, first lieutenant of the *New York* in 1802–03, and as commander of the schooner

Enterprise in 1803–04. As captain of *Enterprise* he captured the Tripolitan warship *Mastico*, which, renamed *Intrepid*, was added to the US Navy.

In October 1803, the American frigate *Philadelphia* ran aground and was captured by the Tripolitans, who refitted it for their navy. But before it could sail, on February 16, 1804 Decatur, with a volunteer assault party aboard *Intrepid*, sailed into the well-fortified harbor. Decatur

This changed in the decades following the Napoleonic era. Improvements in navigation, stronger, larger ships, and steam propulsion reduced the hazards of the sea, permitting well-born incompetents to survive to retirement. But in 1812, birth had not yet replaced merit as the basis for promotion.

Like the seamen, naval officers began their career at a young age, typically in their early teens. Most officers began as "volunteers," carried on the ship's books as one of the captain's servants, typically joining at age 12 to 13. They were actually trainees, learning the basics of seamanship, navigation, and leadership. A British officer candidate might attend the Royal Naval Academy, a form of prep school for future officers. If the youth showed merit, he would be promoted to midshipman.

was able to reach *Philadelphia* and burn the frigate. The action gained Decatur international fame and promotion to captain. Horatio Nelson called it "the most bold and daring act of the age." When Commodore Edward Preble was superseded by Samuel Barron as commander of the Mediterranean squadron in September 1804, Decatur took command of the 44-gun frigate *Constitution* at the age of just 25. He returned to the United States in 1805, after peace with Tripoli was established.

In 1807 Decatur sat on the court martial of James Barron. Barron, sailing to the Mediterranean in command of *Chesapeake*, was stopped by the 50-gun HMS *Leopard* and forced to surrender three crewmen. The court suspended Barron from the US Navy and Decatur took command of *Chesapeake*. With *Chesapeake* and a flotilla of gunboats, Decatur patrolled the American coast to repel any further British attempts to interfere with American shipping.

When the War of 1812 started, Decatur was captain of the *United States*, and sailed with Commodore John Rodgers' squadron to intercept a homeward-bound Jamaica convoy. Rodgers' squadron pursued but failed to catch HMS *Belvidera*, and soon afterward broke up. Shortly afterward, *United States* encountered HMS *Macedonian* and in the battle that followed, reduced *Macedonian* to a hopeless state and captured it. Decatur avoided unnecessarily damaging the British ship once it became apparent that it was not maneuverable. Decatur was able to repair the surrendered frigate, and carry it into New London as a prize.

In August 1814, Decatur transferred to New York City, where he took command of the frigate *President* and New York's naval defenses. In January 1815, Decatur attempted to sail from New York, but *President* grounded leaving harbor, damaging itself. Anticipating where Decatur would go, the commander of the British squadron intercepted *President*. Trapped by the squadron, Decatur was forced to surrender, after a final attempt to escape was blocked by HMS *Endymion*.

Decatur was soon paroled. Following the end of the War of 1812, in 1815 Decatur took command of an American squadron sent to the Mediterranean to again put down the Barbary States. He was present at the capture of the Algerine frigate *Mashuda*, and in concert with a second squadron under the command of William Bainbridge, put an end to the depredations of the Barbary States.

From 1816 to 1820 Decatur served on the Board of Naval Commissioners in Washington DC. In 1820, James Barron challenged Decatur to a duel over comments made about Barron's conduct during the 1807 *Chesapeake–Leopard* incident. Always sensitive on matters of honor, Decatur accepted the challenge. Both officers were badly wounded during the duel, which took place on March 22, and Decatur soon died of his injury. His death helped discredit dueling in the United States.

Midshipman was a warrant rank. The warrant officers occupied an intermediate position in a ship's hierarchy, between the seamen and commissioned officers. There were two broad classes of warrant officers – specialists and trainees.

The specialists included those holding skills vital to a ship's survival – the master (responsible for navigation), boatswain (in charge of rigging and the operations of sailors on deck), carpenter (hull and structure), cooper (stores casks and barrels), and surgeon. The senior warrant officers carried warrants rather than commissions and were permanently assigned to a ship, often forming the core that tended a ship when it was laid up in reserve. Subordinate warrants included midshipmen and mates – assistants to the senior warrants. A master's mate, for example, assisted the master in the navigation of the ship. He held a certificate attesting to his skill in navigation.

The officers' code put a high emphasis on courage and honor. Dueling plagued both navies, but was endemic in the young US Navy, even among junior officers. Here two midshipmen are preparing to exchange shots, probably over a minor slight. Eight years after his victory over *Macedonian* in the War of 1812, Stephen Decatur was slain in a duel. (AC)

Boarding was a last and generally desperate option. Boarders were usually armed with bayoneted muskets and cutlasses, or pistols, boarding pikes and axes. This man is shown standing on a ship's bulkhead railing. He may be preparing either to board an enemy or defend his ship from boarders. (AC)

Midshipmen, as officer candidates, performed many of the functions of the commissioned officers on a smaller scale. They commanded the ship's boats, served as signals officers, or led a section of guns in battle. Older teens, and an occasional man in his twenties, could join the navy with a midshipman's warrant. From midshipman one could progress to either commissioned rank or a master's warrant.

Achieving lieutenancy required a vacancy in that rank. Either one of the lieutenants left the service (often through death) or was promoted, or a lieutenant's position opened as a new ship was commissioned. In the case of an unexpected vacancy, a midshipman or master's mate would be made an acting lieutenant. However, that was a temporary rank. To earn a full lieutenant's commission a candidate had to pass a lieutenant's examination, in which he faced a board of naval captains and demonstrated his ability to discharge a lieutenant's responsibilities. Fail and the candidate reverted to his prior rank. Pass and the coveted commission was received.

The Royal Navy required six years of sea duty before a man could be commissioned as a lieutenant. The US Navy lacked that requirement, and allowed midshipmen to take the lieutenant's examination without a lieutenant's position being open. In such cases, the midshipman became a "passed" midshipman, and would be confirmed as a lieutenant if an opening appeared.

A frigate had three to five lieutenants, whose roles were ordered by seniority. The most senior lieutenant served as the captain's executive officer. The remaining lieutenants each

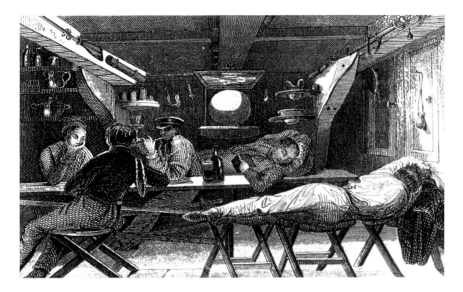

A frigate carried between five and eight midshipmen. They lived in the cockpit, a crowded compartment in the after part of the orlop, below the berth deck. This shows midshipmen in the cockpit, off watch, studying, catching up on sleep or entertaining themselves. (AC)

took one of the ship's watches – running the ship for a two- or four-hour stretch – and were responsible for the gun decks.

From lieutenant, the next step up was commander (more formally, the rank was termed "master and commander"), or more rarely by 1812, directly to captain. A commander commanded a sloop of war: a single-decked warship, smaller than a frigate, which mounted between ten and 24 guns. A full captain, known as a "post captain," commanded "post ships" (ships smaller than frigates but larger than sloops of war), as well as frigates and ships of the line.

Commanders and captains were also ordered by seniority. The length of time a captain had been in rank determined the ship he was given, and whether he was entitled to give orders to others of the same rank, or obliged to take orders from them. In the Royal Navy of 1812, a typical frigate captain had between five and ten years' experience at that rank. More junior captains would generally command post ships, and more senior captains ships of the line. By 1812, US Navy frigate captains typically had a similar level of experience to their British counterparts.

> *His Britannic Majesty's Ship*
> *Shannon off Boston June 1813*
>
> *Sir,*
>
> *As the chesapeake appears now ready for Sea, I request you will do me the favor to meet the Shannon with her, Ship to Ship, to try the fortune of our respective Flags.*

Frigate captains often issued challenges to their opposite numbers. This is a facsimile of a challenge issued by Captain Broke of *Shannon* to James Lawrence of *Chesapeake*. It arrived too late to reach Lawrence, who was already sailing to meet *Shannon*. (AC)

When a British captain reached the top of the captain's list – those above him on it having died or been promoted – he would automatically become an admiral. Both navies then had a temporary rank, above captain but below admiral, called commodore. A captain could be appointed commodore for an specific mission, temporarily givng him superior rank to captains with greater seniority. But in 1812, the US Navy lacked any permanent rank higher than captain, and command of a squadron could be given only to a commodore.

PHILIP BOWES VERE BROKE

Described as being of "an old Suffolk family," Philip Bowes Vere Broke was born at Broke Hall, near Ipswich, in 1779. His background and training were typical of the Royal Navy's frigate captains. Broke entered the navy at the age of 12, attending the Royal Naval Academy at Portsmouth. It was a common age for officers to enter the Royal Navy, although few had Broke's level of formal education, instead going directly to sea as "captain's servants." Broke saw an unusual amount of combat. He was appointed midshipman on the sloop of war *Bulldog* in 1792 and in August 1793 he followed its captain, George Hope, to his new command, *Éclair*. When *Éclair* was sent to the Mediterranean, Broke saw action at the sieges of Toulon and Bastia in 1793 and 1794. He was aboard *Romulus* when Hood's fleet pursued the French at the Gulf of Jouan on June 11, 1794, and was present in actions off Toulon on March 13 and 14, 1794 and July 13, 1794. On July 18, he was appointed third lieutenant of *Southampton*, a frigate. He served on *Southampton* for 18 months, during which time it belonged to then-Commodore Horatio Nelson's squadron off the coast of Italy. He saw action at the battle of Cape St Vincent on February 14, 1797.

Broke returned to Britain when *Southampton* was paid off in June 1797, and was immediately appointed to *Amelia*, another frigate. *Amelia* initially served in the Channel fleet, and participated in the defeat of a French squadron sent to support an invasion of Ireland on October 12, 1798. He gained his promotion to commander on January 2, 1799, and was given the brig of war *Falcon*. Shortly afterwards he was given command of the sloop *Shark* and sent to Duncan's North Sea fleet, where he spent the next two years escorting convoys.

He gained promotion to captain on February 14, 1801. As was typical with many newly-promoted Royal Navy captains, since there were always more captains than post commands, he spent the next four years ashore. Broke's chances of employment were further reduced by the Peace of Amiens. Signed in March 1802, this treaty briefly ended the long war between France and Britain. Shortly afterward, in September 1802, Broke married, and with his wife Sarah he was to have 11 children. Broke finally returned to sea in April 1805, when he was appointed captain of the frigate *Druid*. He commanded *Druid* for 18 months, serving in the Channel and off Ireland. On August 31, 1806, Broke was given command of *Shannon*. The frigate had been launched in May, and sailed on August 3, 1806. He was to command *Shannon* for the next seven years.

As *Shannon*'s captain, Broke gained a reputation for initiative. He also was considered eccentric, due to his emphasis on gunnery. Broke not only drilled his men on the guns daily, but regularly conducted live-fire practice with floating targets, and he also fitted the guns with sights so that they would hit where they were aimed. Broke personally paid for both the practice gunpowder and gun sights. *Shannon* initially served in the Baltic in 1807, then in the reduction of Madeira, and in the Bay of Biscay from 1808 through 1811. With tensions with the United States rising, *Shannon* was transferred to the North America station in August 1811.

Broke spent the first year of the War of 1812 seeking an American frigate. To keep *Shannon* fully manned, he burned prizes rather than send men away in prize crews. His patience was rewarded in May 1813, when he met *Chesapeake* off Boston Harbor. After a brutal 15-minute battle, Broke defeated and captured the American frigate; the first and only Royal Navy captain to do so in the conflict.

Following this victory, Broke was showered with honors. He was made a baronet in 1813, a Knight Commander of the Order of Bath in 1815, and was awarded a Navy Gold Medal. But Broke's career effectively ended with the capture of *Chesapeake.* During the battle he received a severe head injury, from which he never fully recovered. His injuries were compounded by a fall from a horse in 1820, which left him unfit for active duty.

He remained in the Royal Navy, and was frequently consulted on issues of naval gunnery for the rest of his career. He lived to be promoted to rear admiral in July 1830, and died in London on January 2, 1841.

COMBAT

Four frigate duels were fought during the War of 1812, all in the first 12 months following the US Congress' declaration of war. The first three pitted an American 24-pounder frigate against a British 18-pounder ship, and the final duel was fought between two frigates with 18-pounder batteries, and virtually identical broadside weights.

CONSTITUTION vs *GUERRIERE*

Captain Isaac Hull was having a bad war. He had taken his command, the 44-gun frigate *Constitution*, in search of Commodore John Rodgers' squadron, which Hull was to join. Instead of finding his squadron, he stumbled across the ships of the Royal Navy's entire North America station – a 64-gun ship of the line, four frigates and a captured American sloop of war. Hull had escaped – barely – but had been forced to throw his fresh water overboard to lighten ship, necessitating a return to port. In Boston, he was greeted with the news that his uncle, General William Hull, had surrendered an American army in Detroit. There were rumors he was to be relieved of *Constitution*'s command.

Hull hastily took on stores and fled to sea before the rumors became reality. Still seeking Rodgers and his squadron, on August 18 off Cape Race he encountered an American privateer. The privateer's captain told him of a lone British frigate to the south. Hull sailed in chase and was rewarded when, at 2pm the next day, a sail was spotted to leeward, east-southeast. It proved to be *Guerrière*, a British 38-gun frigate commanded by Captain James Dacres.

Dacres, too, was having a frustrating war. Having achieved a captain's dream – a frigate command – he had then been assigned to American waters. Not to the Caribbean,

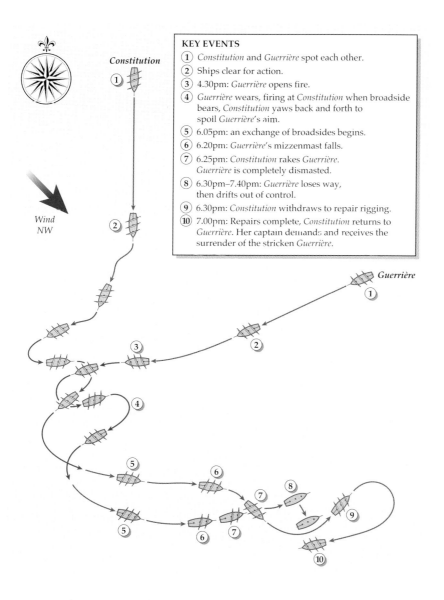

KEY EVENTS

1. *Constitution* and *Guerrière* spot each other.
2. Ships clear for action.
3. 4.30pm: *Guerrière* opens fire.
4. *Guerrière* wears, firing at *Constitution* when broadside bears, *Constitution* yaws back and forth to spoil *Guerrière*'s aim.
5. 6.05pm: an exchange of broadsides begins.
6. 6.20pm: *Guerrière*'s mizzenmast falls.
7. 6.25pm: *Constitution* rakes *Guerrière*. *Guerrière* is completely dismasted.
8. 6.30pm–7.40pm: *Guerrière* loses way, then drifts out of control.
9. 6.30pm: *Constitution* withdraws to repair rigging.
10. 7.00pm: Repairs complete, *Constitution* returns to *Guerrière*. Her captain demands and receives the surrender of the stricken *Guerrière*.

Constitution

Guerrière

Wind
NW

swarming with privateers and prizes, but Halifax and the North America station – as quiet a posting as was possible in a world at war. He spent time socializing with his American counterparts instead of fighting the French and Spanish. Now war with the United States offered an opportunity for distinction, but so far, *Guerrière* had only participated in a frustrating chase of *Constitution*, the ship now approaching from windward.

Hull and Dacres had debated the merits of their respective ships in prewar days. Dacres believed that the handier *Guerrière* could best the Yankee frigate. Despite its heavier battery, the enemy ship had to be too large for nimble maneuvering, and except in heavy winds, was bound to be slower. Dacres wanted to fight an American frigate. *Guerrière* routinely stopped any ship it encountered, and if it belonged to a neutral nation, Dacres asked its captain to pass a message to any Yankee frigates it

49

met: *Guerrière* was sailing to the Sandy Hook and would be willing to meet any US Navy frigate in single combat there.

Now there was his opportunity to capture the first American frigate of the war – and the enemy was upwind of him. Dacres wanted to fight, but if his foe did not, it would be a long chase. Dacres also had another worry. In January, *Guerrière* had been surveyed, and the shipwrights had recommended that *Guerrière's* masts be renewed within six months. But eight months later, they had still not been replaced.

Dacres ordered his ship to quarters, and the frigate's elaborate ritual of preparing for battle began. The ship's drummer beat a long, rolling tattoo – the signal for the crew to "beat to quarters." Everything that was not needed to fight and survive was removed to the hold. Partitions were disassembled and taken below, along with benches, tables, and anything else that would turn into a storm of flying splinters if struck by a cannonball.

The crew assembled at their stations for battle. Marines took their places in the fighting tops and along the ship's bulwarks. The gunner retired to the ship's magazine, where he would dole out cartridges filled with measured amounts of gunpowder to the waiting powder boys, who would carry them to the guns. Curtains in the magazine were doused with water, and the gunner wore felt slippers to reduce the chance of a spark igniting the magazine.

The guns were cast loose from the ship's bulwarks, where they were normally secured, and made ready for action. Tompions were removed from the muzzles and sponge tubs filled with salt water, so that guns could be swabbed out after each round was fired, dousing the remaining embers before a fresh charge was inserted. To improve sailors' footing on decks that might soon be running with blood, the decks were wetted and sprinkled with sand.

The royal yards and masts were struck – taken down – to reduce the strain on the masts. Chain slings were attached to spars to keep them from crashing to the deck, if the rigging holding them was parted by shot. The ship's boats were often removed from their places on the ship's decks and put into the water, again to reduce sources of splinters. The boats were either cut loose, with a few men to tend them, or towed behind the ship.

A ship could beat to quarters in as little as ten minutes, although that often entailed throwing partitions and furniture overboard. More generally if time permitted – as it would have on this occasion – it would take 20 to 30 minutes.

With his ship preparing for battle, Dacres attempted to gain the weather gage – the favorable position to windward of his foe. To ease the strain on his masts, he wore ship, turning with the wind. Tacking, or turning into the wind, was faster, but put his old masts at risk. On *Constitution*, Hull was equally eager for combat. The big American frigate beat to quarters, and switched to battle sail. Captain Hull took in his courses, struck the royal masts and spars, and furled the topgallants.

By this time, it was 4.30pm. The wind was from the northwest, and *Constitution* lay almost directly upwind of *Guerrière*. Dacres, abandoning his effort to gain the weather gage, also shifted to battle sail, and backed his main topsail, challenging his opponent to fight. As *Constitution* ran downwind towards the British frigate, Dacres opened fire at extreme range. But the range was too great and his first broadside fell short. He wore ship, and fired his port broadside. But *Constitution* had closed the range, and *Guerrière's* broadside went high.

The first broadside fired was more effective than subsequent broadsides. It was carefully loaded, and generally the best aimed. Once a ship was in the midst of battle, rounds were loaded and fired quickly, since good gunnery was thought to be measured by a ship's volume of fire, even at the expense of careful aim. *Guerrière's* crew could reload and fire in 40 seconds, but Dacres had now spent the first broadside's advantage to no effect.

As Hull ran down on *Guerrière*, he yawed *Constitution* repeatedly, following a zigzag course to his foe. This spoiled *Guerrière's* aim, and denied Dacres the opportunity for a raking shot – one that hit the bow or the stern head-on and smashed down the length of a ship. Hull's approach took 90 minutes, during which time *Guerrière* continued wearing, while *Constitution*, reserving its broadside, fired an occasional bow chaser. By 6pm, running before the wind, *Constitution* reached *Guerrière*. Dacres too wore his ship to sail before the wind, and *Constitution* came up *Guerrière's* larboard side. At 6.05pm, broadside-to-broadside at pistol shot range (30 yards) the two ships opened fire.

Constitution proved faster than *Guerrière* when both were under topsails, and was slowly pulling ahead of *Guerrière*. *Guerrière* fired faster than *Constitution*, but to less effect. After a 15-minute exchange of broadsides, *Guerrière* had suffered significant damage, while *Constitution* was virtually unhurt. At 6.20pm, *Guerrière's* mizzenmast fell, falling to starboard, and fouling the ship. With this, *Guerrière* had lost its ability to maneuver or escape.

Seizing his advantage, Hull sailed *Constitution* in front of *Guerrière*, placing *Constitution* broadside to *Guerrière's* bow. The ships were so close that *Guerrière's* bowsprit hung over *Constitution's* deck. The *Constitution's* guns, at a range too close to miss, fired down the full length of *Guerrière's* decks, killing men, dismounting guns, and smashing timbers.

Dacres realized his remaining hope of victory lay in boarding and taking his foe. He went forward to organize a boarding party. Hull, too, ordered boarders, forming his party on *Constitution's* quarterdeck. This proved the bloodiest part of the action. Both ships had sharpshooters on the rails and in the fighting tops, who took advantage of the close range to rain fire down on their opponents.

But capturing *Constitution* through boarding was unrealistic. *Constitution's* crew was 60 percent larger than *Guerrière's*, and had taken no casualties prior to the exchange of musketry, whereas *Guerrière's* crew had suffered significantly in the exchange of broadsides and the murderous raking fire. Further handicapping the British ship was the fact that ten members of *Guerrière's* crew were American, who had refused to fight against their own country, and who had been sent below prior to the battle. But slim as it was, boarding was the only chance Dacres had, so he it took it.

Officers were always prime targets for musketry, and this battle was no exception. *Constitution's* lieutenant of marines was killed, and its first lieutenant and master were wounded. On *Guerrière*, Dacres was shot from *Constitution's* mizzentop, and other American marines hit two of *Guerrière's* lieutenants and the master.

This painting, the first in a series of four painted by Michel Felice Corne for Isaac Hull to commemorate the battle between *Constitution* and *Guerrière,* shows the two ships at the start of the battle. *Constitution* is changing to battle sail, while *Guerrière* waits, its main topsail backed in challenge. (USNHF)

Neither side boarded. *Guerrière*'s foremast and mainmast, battered by raking fire, fell just as Dacres was ready to order boarders away, and clearing away the dangerous wreckage suddenly took priority. On *Constitution,* Hull realized boarding was now unnecessary. Instead, at 6.30pm, he pulled his ship away from the dismasted *Guerrière,* and stood to leeward, where he spent 15 minutes repairing damage to the rigging.

Hull's first priority was to make *Constitution* ready for another potential battle. The Royal Navy had ships everywhere, so Hull could not assume that he would not be interrupted by another British warship. Indeed, just two months later the American sloop of war *Wasp* would be captured unprepared by HMS *Poictiers,* having just

With *Guerrière* crippled by the loss of its mizzen, *Constitution* sails in front of *Guerrière*'s bow and unleashes a devastating raking broadside. Note the backed mizzen topsail, intended to slow *Constitution* while slewing the stern to larboard, thus increasing the effectiveness of the rake. (USNHF)

The second painting in the series shows the battle at 6.20pm. The ships have traded broadsides for 15 minutes, and *Constitution* has succeeded in shooting away *Guerrière*'s mizzenmast. (USNHF)

defeated HMS *Frolic*. The British ship of the line, attracted by the sound of gunfire, caught *Wasp* before the sloop could repair its battle-damaged masts.

Having repaired his ship, Hull then returned to the scene of the battle, reaching *Guerrière* at 7pm. By then it was dark, and Hull could not tell whether *Guerrière* had struck its colors. He sent a lieutenant across to *Guerrière* in a boat to inquire as to the British ship's status.

Guerrière was a dismasted, rolling hulk, incapable of fighting, and Dacres surrendered his ship without further combat. Of its crew of 272 men, more than 25 percent were casualties, with 23 dead and 56 wounded. (*Constitution* had suffered

Having retired to repair rigging, *Constitution* returns to the dismasted *Guerrière* to demand its surrender. Because of British maritime supremacy, prudent American captains set their ship to rights before taking possession of a prize. (USNHF)

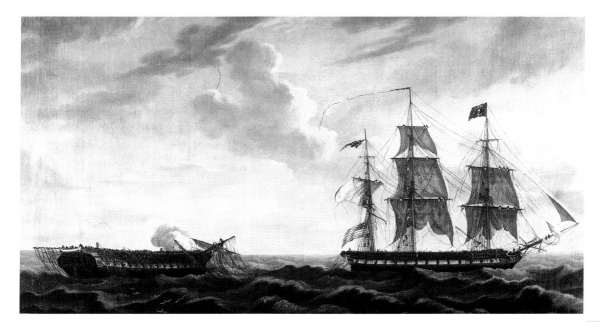

just seven killed and seven wounded.) The *Constitution*'s 24-pounder guns had wrought terrible damage to *Guerrière*'s structural timbers.

Constitution's third lieutenant, George Read, was sent aboard *Guerrière* as prize master. By the next morning, he reported that *Guerrière* was in danger of sinking. Hull quickly decided that taking the ship into port as a prize was impractical. He evacuated the British crew to *Constitution*, and at 3pm *Guerrière* was set alight. The frigate exploded when the fire reached her magazine.

Hull returned in triumph to Boston, where he unloaded his prisoners. The orders relieving him of command caught up with him, but he had already achieved the glory to which frigate captains aspired.

The battle between *Constitution* and *Guerrière* was the first major naval engagement of the War of 1812. The news shocked the British, who since 1794 had regularly defeated French 24-pounder frigates, and had grown accustomed to victory. Defeating the world's maritime superpower proved a tonic to the United States, which had been discouraged by reverses by land in Canada. It also set the pattern for the next two frigate duels in the War of 1812.

UNITED STATES vs *MACEDONIAN*

As dawn broke on October 25, 1812, two frigates spotted each other in the north Atlantic near the Azores. To the southwest was *Macedonian*, rated 38 guns and commanded by John Surnam Carden. To the northeast was *United States*, a Humphreys 44, with Captain

Stephen Decatur commanding. Both captains were eager for battle – Carden to avenge the loss of *Guerrière*, and Decatur to prove that *Constitution*'s victory had been no fluke.

Both ships had been in commission long enough for their crews to be fully trained. *Macedonian* was considered a crack ship, and in terms of sail handling and dumb-show gunnery drill – practice at running the guns out, mock-firing, and reloading – it certainly was. But Carden was both unimaginative and a martinet, and *Macedonian*'s crew was dispirited. Moreover, Carden rarely held live-fire practice with his guns.

In contrast, Decatur, one of the true leaders of the age of sail, had trained his crew superbly. While not a picked crew – they had been recruited from available manpower – they were now well drilled and highly motivated. Unlike *Macedonian*, Decatur's ship frequently expended powder and shot during gunnery practice.

Carden approached his opponent directly, but cautiously. He held the weather gage, the upwind position, and was determined to hold it. He believed his opponent was *Essex*, a 32-gun frigate, much smaller than *Macedonian* and armed primarily with carronades. *United States* beat to windward to reach *Macedonian*. At 8.30am, with *Macedonian* just out of gunshot, Decatur wore *United States*, putting it on a course where it would cross *Macedonian*'s bow. Determined to keep the weather gage, Carden turned slightly to starboard. Seeing his attempt checked, Decatur wore again, back to his original course of west-southwest. The two ships passed each other on parallel courses, out of range of one another.

Once past *United States*, Carden wore ship, turning *Macedonian* 180 degrees, and set his frigate on a course converging with that of *United States*. Decatur jogged slightly to starboard to open the range, then resumed his original course. With a 24-pounder battery, heavier than the 18-pounders mounted by *Macedonian*, Decatur was willing to fight at extended range.

By the time the ships were within range, it was 9.45am. Battle commenced with a 15-minute exchange of long-range broadsides, with both ships only able to use their great guns. The 24lb balls slamming into *Macedonian* told Carden his opponent was

OVERLEAF

This shows what James Dacres would have seen at 6.15pm. *Guerrière* has been exchanging broadsides with *Constitution* for 15 minutes. During that time, *Guerrière* has fired 22 broadsides into the American frigate with little apparent effect. Few shots are hitting and none seem to be doing much damage. Indeed, several of the 18lb balls have bounced straight off *Constitution*, and Dacres is becoming aware of the chaos developing on his ship. The American's shot is smashing bulwarks and dismounting guns. Sharpshooters in *Constitution*'s tops are also cutting down his men, although even at 30 yards, a hit requires more luck than skill.

The worst piece of fortune is now occurring, literally over Dacres' head. A shot from *Constitution*, probably from a 32-pounder carronade on the quarterdeck, has struck the mizzenmast, snapping it 10ft above the deck. With its mizzenmast broken and dragging in the water *Guerrière* cannot steer, and the ship is doomed.

not *Essex*, and of the two ships, *United States* had both the higher rate of fire and more accurate gunnery. With lighter guns and a crew who lacked real gunnery experience, *Macedonian*'s return broadsides were ineffectual at long range. In addition, Decatur was ahead of *Macedonian*, forcing Carden to use only his forward guns.

In this position, Carden's percentage move would have been to break off the action and attempt another approach, seeking a more advantageous position. Instead, Carden now compounded the mistake of his initially timid approach by rashly closing with *United States*. Carden set his forecourse to increase *Macedonian*'s speed, and overhaul *United States*.

Decatur was equal to the challenge. Through skillful ship handling, Decatur maintained *United States*'s position off *Macedonian*'s port quarter, and over the next half hour, *United States* picked *Macedonian* to pieces. Mizzen topmast, main yard, and main topsail went by the board, the forward carronades were all dismounted, and then the mizzenmast and both remaining topmasts fell. Finally, *United States* crossed the stricken *Macedonian*'s bow, but did not fire the expected raking broadside. Instead, Decatur sailed out of *Macedonian*'s field of fire to repair its damaged rigging.

Once repairs were complete, Decatur again took *United States* across the stationary *Macedonian*'s bow and waited, without firing. Having demonstrated the helplessness of his foe, Decatur called upon Carden to surrender. Some hotheads aboard *Macedonian* advocated fighting on, but reasonable heads prevailed. *Macedonian* struck her colors at 11.15am. Of the 301 men aboard *Macedonian,* 43 were dead or mortally wounded, and 61 were injured. *United States* had lost seven killed and five wounded.

Due to Decatur's forbearance, *Macedonian*'s hull was still sound. Decatur gave his first lieutenant, James Allen, command of the prize, and decided to take it home. Jury-rigged masts were set and, with *United States* in escort, *Macedonian* reached New London, Connecticut on December 4.

One of the US Navy's most senior captains in 1812, William Bainbridge had a reputation as an unlucky officer and a harsh disciplinarian. But he was a competent seaman and fighter. (LOC)

CONSTITUTION vs JAVA

At 9am on December 29, 1812, *Constitution* was cruising off the coast of Brazil, when it spotted two sail. *Constitution*'s captain was now William Bainbridge, one of the US Navy's most senior captains. The sail proved to be HMS *Java*, six weeks out of Spithead, in company with *William*, an American merchant prize. *Java* was another French prize, a fast ship, armed with a standard battery for a British 38-gun frigate. She was sailing to reinforce Britain's East Indies squadron, and carried supplies and reinforcements. As a result, she had a large contingent of supernumeraries, and in total she had 426 men aboard.

Bainbridge wanted to fight *Java*, but not in Portuguese territorial waters. He tacked, and ran to seaward. *Java* followed. Captain Henry Lambert, commanding *Java*, had a fast ship, a sound hull, and a good crew. He was eager to demonstrate that the two earlier British defeats were simply bad luck.

The pursuit continued for two hours. *Java* proved a faster ship than *Constitution*, reaching ten knots during the chase. By then, the ships had a sufficient distance from the Brazilian coast, and both ships cleared for action. Battle commenced at 2pm, when *Constitution* fired a ranging shot at 800 yards. *Java* held the weather gage, and placed herself off *Constitution*'s larboard bow. Both ships wore, exchanging broadsides at long range. *Java*'s gunnery was better than that of *Guerrière* or *Macedonian*, and at 2.30pm, *Java* shot away *Constitution*'s wheel, leaving the big frigate unmaneuverable and temporarily at *Java*'s mercy. *Java* fired a broadside at *Constitution*'s stern, but this raking shot, so deadly when accurate, had little effect. As the battle continued, the quality of *Java*'s gunnery was worsening.

Having survived the rake, Bainbridge regained the helm, and the two ships maneuvered to exchange broadsides at 400 yards. *Constitution*'s heavier broadside and *Java*'s deteriorating gunnery told, and just before 3pm, *Java*'s bowsprit was carried away. Deprived of the headsails needed to maneuver the ship, *Java* was in trouble. Retaining his large crew of sailors and supernumeraries, Lambert attempted to retrieve the situation by boarding. But as he attempted the turn to close with the American frigate, the maneuver caused the ship's damaged foremast to fall. *Java* drifted into *Constitution*, fouling *Constitution*'s mizzen with the stump of the bowsprit.

Constitution pulled free before the British could use the bowsprit to board, then sailed across *Java*'s stern. *Constitution*'s raking broadside at half-pistol shot tore away *Java*'s main topmast, and mortally wounded Captain Lambert. It also damaged *Java*'s mizzenmast, which collapsed at 4.35pm. With his enemy helpless – only *Java*'s main course could be set – Bainbridge retired to repair his rigging. He returned at 5.30pm, and placed *Constitution* across *Java*'s bow. Further resistance being useless, Henry Ducie Chads, *Java*'s senior surviving lieutenant, surrendered.

Java had every advantage an 18-pounder frigate could expect. She had the weather gage, and could choose the moment of engagement. Her crew was good and almost as large as *Constitution*'s, and Henry Lambert was a more capable captain than either Dacres or Carden. Finally, *Constitution* carried two fewer 32-pounder carronades than when it fought *Guerrière*, and had the disadvantage of a new crew. When Bainbridge took command, most of Hull's crew had followed him ashore.

None of this mattered. Although the battle fought was the hardest one *Constitution* would experience, the end result was the same: a British frigate was a badly damaged, dismasted hulk. *Java* had 48 men killed or mortally wounded, and 102 men injured in the battle. Just 12 members of *Constitution*'s crew died as a result of the battle and 22 others were wounded.

The battle between *Constitution* and *Java* ended virtually the same way as the first two frigate duels, with the British ship dismasted and at the mercy of its American foe. Had *Java*'s gunnery been better, it could have ended differently. (USNAM)

Due to the damage his prize had suffered, and the distance to an American port, Bainbridge ordered *Java* sunk the next day. He landed and paroled the 378 surviving prisoners at neutral Bahai, in Brazil, and cut short *Constitution*'s South Atlantic cruise to return to the United States for repairs and stores. *Constitution* would spend the next year in Boston Harbor.

CHESAPEAKE vs *SHANNON*

A year's worth of American victories had shaken Great Britain out of complacency. Fortune's favors were no longer considered to be British by birthright. The Royal Navy was recommissioning the 24-pounder frigates it had laid up, and was building new, larger super-frigates to match the Humphreys 24-pounder design. The Admiralty had also sent orders not to fight the American 44-gun frigates one-on-one. Britain had an overwhelming advantage in numbers, and was now prepared to use it.

The Americans had now become as complacent as the Royal Navy in June 1812. Six successful single-ship duels occurred that first year, three involving frigates, and three involving sloops of war. The American public expected American naval victories.

No US Navy officer had more contempt for the quality of Royal Navy officers than James Lawrence, and with good reason. In January 1813, while commanding the sloop of war *Hornet*, Lawrence had won a crushing victory over HMS *Peacock*, an 18-gun *Cruizer*-class brig. Its captain, Commander William Peake, treated *Peacock* as a social tool rather than a warship, to the point where his fellow officers nicknamed it "The Yacht." Peake valued comfort and appearance over fighting ability, even to the point of exchanging the sloop's regulation 32-pounder carronades for 24-pounders. The smaller weapons allowed more room for entertaining.

Lawrence's victory earned him promotion to captain, and command of *Chesapeake*. Rated at 44 guns when launched, and designed to carry 18-pounder long guns,

Through skillful handling, Stephen Decatur placed *United States* off *Macedonian*'s starboard bow, and kept the two ships in that position. This Currier and Ives print of the battle shows it at an intermediate point, as *United States* slowly batters *Macedonian* to pieces. (LOC)

Chesapeake had been re-rated as a 36-gun frigate after 1808. It was the smallest 36-gun frigate in the US Navy, virtually identical in size and armament to a British 38-gun frigate.

The ship was at Boston when Lawrence took command on May 20, following an unsuccessful cruise in 1812. Most of the crew were experienced sailors. Many were foreign-born, including 40 from Britain (who were committing treason by voluntarily taking up arms against their homeland) and a large contingent of Portuguese. It was not a bad crew, but the men had never worked together. *Chesapeake*'s two junior lieutenants were acting officers, midshipmen temporarily promoted to lieutenant. In less than two weeks, Lawrence made *Chesapeake* ready for sea, and ready for the ship that lay in wait.

Outside Boston harbor lay HMS *Shannon*, a *Leda*-class 38, commanded by Philip Broke. Broke and his ship had been in American waters for almost two years. In May

After dismasting *Macedonian*, Decatur sailed *United States* across the 38-gun frigate's bow, but did not fire. Having demonstrated that *Macedonian* was helpless, Decatur retired to repair rigging before returning to take possession of his prize. (FDRL)

1813, *Shannon* was overdue to return to England, but Broke had been putting off his return to Halifax where he expected recall orders to quash his hopes of fighting an American frigate. He was also aware that *Chesapeake* was ready to put to sea. Confident of victory, and desperate for an opportunity to fight, Broke sent a personal, written challenge to *Chesapeake*'s captain to meet *Shannon* in single combat.

This was a gamble. Technically, he was under orders not to fight a single-ship action with American frigates; but Broke felt victory would erase any insubordination, and his ship was unusually ready for combat. Unlike *Guerrière*, *Macedonian*, and *Java*, *Shannon* regularly conducted live-fire target practice. *Shannon* could even aim when the gunners were blinded by smoke, as the guns had markings on the decks around them, allowing the gun captains to aim on an azimuth called down from the fighting tops.

Broke's note was delivered on June 1, 1813, as *Chesapeake* was sailing. Lawrence never received it, and headed to his planned rendezvous ignorant of the invitation. He intended to become the first American captain since Thomas Truxton to defeat two enemy warships, and the first one ever to capture two. Basing his standard for British seamanship and naval leadership on the *Peacock* and Commander William Peake, Lawrence believed he could win an easy victory, despite a green American crew.

In June 1812, Royal Navy officers believed two British sailors were worth three Americans, four Frenchmen or six Spaniards. In June 1813, Lawrence reversed the conceit, certain that two Americans were worth three, or even four British seamen.

The weather was almost perfect for a battle. There was a fresh breeze, allowing the ships to sail and maneuver freely, but the wind was not so strong as to throw up rough seas and affect gunnery. *Chesapeake* cleared the Boston lighthouse at 1pm. Twenty miles offshore, *Shannon* lay to under battle sail, with topsails and topgallants set. It was 4pm.

Chesapeake sailed directly for her opponent under a full press of sail, including studdingsails. At 5pm *Chesapeake* took in her studdingsails and struck her royal masts and yards, switching to battle sail. The breeze freshened, and *Chesapeake* was flying

In January 1813, Lawrence, commanding sloop of war USS *Hornet*, quickly took HMS *Peacock*. The easy victory led Lawrence to underestimate the Royal Navy. (USNHF)

along under topsails and jibs alone. At 5.25pm, *Chesapeake* altered course to go straight at *Shannon*, which was almost directly downwind. By 5.30pm, Broke realized that he had misjudged *Chesapeake*'s position, and that he was at risk of having *Chesapeake* cross *Shannon*'s stern. Broke ordered *Shannon*'s main topsail backed, to slow the ship, and reduce *Chesapeake*'s opportunity for a rake.

Broke need not have worried. Lawrence, foregoing the rake, which would have cost him the weather gage, luffed up as he came within 50 yards of *Shannon*'s starboard stern quarter, and sailed a course parallel to his opponent. It was 5.45pm.

Five minutes later, both ships opened fire, and for the next ten minutes both ships furiously exchanged broadsides at pistol-shot range. *Chesapeake*'s gunnery was good, 50 rounds striking *Shannon*'s hull and masts during those ten minutes. Most of the casualties that *Shannon* suffered during the battle – 33 men killed and 50 wounded – were hit during that period.

But *Shannon*'s gunnery was superb. *Chesapeake* was hit 81 times, cutting down James Lawrence, who was taken below mortally wounded, and several of the afterguard on the quarterdeck. Casualties were also heavy on the gun deck, demoralizing the ship's green crew.

Chesapeake's agony was compounded when a grenade tossed from *Shannon*'s fighting tops landed on a quarterdeck arms chest. The explosion cleared *Chesapeake*'s quarterdeck, leaving it temporarily unmanned. Uninjured survivors were shocked into a stupor. Simultaneously, stray shots from *Shannon* sliced the spanker brail aft and the jib's sheet forward. The spanker came down and filled, while the jib flapped uselessly.

The breeze forced *Chesapeake*'s stern to windward. Unchecked by a restraining force at the bow – previously provided by the now-missing jib – *Chesapeake* pivoted. Its stern swung round towards *Shannon*. With no one at the helm to restrain the

Lawrence was hit and mortally wounded during the gunnery exchange. In a romanticized nineteenth century print, Lawrence is being carried below to the surgeon. The picture has several anachronisms, including a boarding battle in progress, sailors in uniform and quarterdeck long guns instead of carronades. (FDRL)

COULD *CHESAPEAKE* HAVE WON?

On paper, no frigate duel in the War of 1812 was closer than that between *Chesapeake and Shannon*. But the disparity in crew quality and leadership gave *Shannon* a decisive edge. With Broke's exemplary leadership and a well-drilled crew that had worked together for seven years, *Shannon* would have been a challenge for even a *Constitution*-class frigate. That is not to say that *Chesapeake*'s defeat was inevitable. If it had been Stephen Decatur who commanded *Chesapeake* on that fateful day, it is likely that the battle would have played out differently.

Firstly, it is likely that the battle would not have taken place. Experienced leaders — like Hull, Decatur, and Rodgers — respected their opponents. Decatur would likely not have challenged any Royal Navy warship until his crew was trained to his satisfaction. He would have avoided combat and instead spent the next two weeks drilling his crew.

Had he been unable to avoid combat, Decatur would have fought a smarter battle than Lawrence. Although given the opportunity to open the battle with a devastating stern rake, Lawrence opted to trade broadsides with *Shannon*, yardarm-to-yardarm. Decatur would have instead seized the moment. The effect of a well-aimed opening broadside entering the unprotected stern and sweeping the length of the gun decks could disorganize and demoralize even an elite crew.

But there would still have been no guarantee of victory. Even a Decatur could not have welded *Chesapeake*'s crew into a unified fighting force in two weeks, and the superior gunnery and discipline of *Shannon* might still have given Broke victory.

---

motion, *Chesapeake*'s quarter gallery struck *Shannon* amidships, fouling on a spare anchor stored there. It was now 6pm. Broke suddenly found *Chesapeake*, its quarterdeck empty, locked to *Shannon*, and seized the opportunity. Calling for his crew to follow, he boarded *Chesapeake*.

It was not an organized boarding party, but a motley crew of those who heard and followed their captain's call. Just 20 men boarded, but it was enough. The demoralized survivors on the spar deck panicked and fled below. Of *Chesapeake*'s marine contingent, only ten remained uninjured, but dazed, on the quarterdeck. They resisted but were overwhelmed. *Chesapeake*'s third lieutenant, who had carried Lawrence below, had just returned to the quarterdeck. He too panicked and ran below.

American marksmen in *Chesapeake*'s tops tried to clear the boarders, but were soon driven from their positions. Broke had been badly injured in the boarding, but the British were now in possession of the entire spar deck.

The gun deck crews, led by Lieutenant George Budd, commanding the main battery, now attempted to storm the spar deck. They killed several of the British, but were beaten back. Now reinforced from *Shannon*, the British boarding party began firing muskets down the hatches. Further resistance was futile, and Budd, the senior surviving officer, surrendered *Chesapeake*. It was 6.05pm. The battle had lasted just 15 minutes.

American casualties were heavy. Sixty-one men were killed or mortally wounded, and 81 others injured. Every commissioned officer aboard *Chesapeake* had been either killed or wounded, as were most of the warrant and petty officers. *Shannon* also took a heavy butcher's bill, suffering more casualties in victory than *Guerrière* had in defeat.

Shannon carried *Chesapeake* into Halifax harbor in triumph. Broke became the hero of the hour, the man who redeemed Britain's honor. In death, Lawrence achieved legendary status. His dying words were "Don't give up the ship." It became the US Navy's rallying cry.

STATISTICS AND ANALYSIS

Napoleon once claimed that "God is on the side with the best artillery." If not God, then fortune certainly favored the side with the heaviest battery in the War of 1812. In three of the four frigate duels that were fought, the victorious ship had a decisive advantage in broadside metal. Yet it would be more accurate to say that fortune favored the prepared, for the better-trained and better-drilled crew won all four encounters.

Table 1 shows the relative firepower in each battle. The superiority ratio is a ship's broadside weight divided by its opponent's broadside weight. In the first three the victorious US Navy frigate had a decisive advantage in firepower, and in the battle between *Shannon* and *Chesapeake* the difference was so small as to be negligible.

More significant than the weight of metal is the percentage of shot that actually struck home. By 1812, the Royal Navy had been continuously at war since 1793, and over that period, British frigates routinely bested larger French and Spanish opponents, often at odds longer than those faced against the Humphreys frigates. Superior British gunnery had been the key to those victories.

When the war with America broke out, Britain had not been seriously challenged at sea since 1806. As a result, especially on quiet stations such as North America, gunnery had taken second place to seamanship and smartness. Few British captains conducted live-fire practice, either firing blank charges or shooting at real, floating targets. Those that did, like Broke, paid for the practice gunpowder and shot themselves, and were considered somewhat eccentric by their contemporaries. For most captains at the time, gunnery drill consisted of running the guns in and out until crews became familiar with the mechanics of firing the guns.

Table 1: Relative firepower

Battle	Ship	Broadside weight of metal at battle (pounds)	Superiority ratio
Constitution vs Guerrière, **August 19, 1812**	Constitution	736	1.37
	Guerrière	538	0.73
United States vs **Macedonian, October 30,** **1812**	United States	846	1.60
	Macedonian	529	0.63
Constitution vs Java, **December 29, 1812**	Constitution	704	1.28
	Java	552	0.78
Chesapeake vs Shannon, **June 1, 1813**	Chesapeake	552	1.05
	Shannon	526	0.95

Three broadsides every two minutes was the standard. Yet unless the crews were given realistic gunnery practice, firing at floating targets with live ammunition, their ability to actually hit anything – even at minimal ranges – was negligible.

The results of this weakness are particularly clear in *Constitution*'s battles with *Guerrière* and *Java*. *Guerrière* fired numerous broadsides at *Constitution* during *Constitution*'s 90-minute approach. *Guerrière* had time to aim each broadside, and was opposed only by *Constitution*'s two bow chasers. Yet *Guerrière* failed to do any significant damage. Tellingly, the first broadside *Guerrière* fired once *Constitution* was in range went over *Constitution*. *Guerrière*'s gun crews probably fired high throughout the battle.

OVERLEAF
At 6.15pm Captain Isaac Hull of *Constitution* is observing the progress of his battle from *his* quarterdeck. His view is far more satisfactory than Captain Dacres', seen on pages 56–57. The two ships have been trading broadsides for 15 minutes, and Hull's 24-pounder main battery and 32-pounder spar deck carronades are demolishing *Guerrière*.
Constitution has received little damage so far, and no casualties. *Guerrière* is firing at a tremendous rate, but the sound and fury seems to be signifying nothing. The few balls that do strike home do not penetrate. The hands, seeing this, give *Constitution* its enduring nickname – "Old Ironsides."
Constitution is slowly but steadily pulling ahead of *Guerrière*. Once his ship forereaches *Guerrière*, Hull intends to cross his opponent's bows and rake it. *Guerrière*'s mizzenmast is damaged and falling, and it will fall foul on its starboard side, serving to anchor the ship where it lies. *Guerrière* will lose speed and maneuverability, and victory is now within Hull's grasp.

The broadside duel between *Constitution* and *Guerrière* lasted 15 minutes. At a rate of fire of 40 seconds per round – the standard to which Dacres held his crew – *Guerrière* could have fired as many as 560 rounds at *Constitution* during this period. Even at a slower rate, it can be assumed that *Guerrière* sent at least 300 rounds at a target no more than 30 yards away. *Constitution* was a target 175ft long and 18ft high, an area of 350 square yards. Not one of the shots *Guerrière* fired during that interval penetrated *Constitution*'s side.

Java's lack of gunnery proved even more costly. Lambert got every frigate captain's dream: a raking broadside into his disabled opponent's unprotected stern at close range. Such a broadside, properly aimed, could decide a battle; but *Java*'s rake failed to hurt *Constitution*. Most of the shots missed and *Java* got no second chance at victory.

By contrast, every American captain conducted live-fire practice. Decatur had held command of *United States* for over a year when he fought *Macedonian*; Hull had commanded *Constitution* for three months. Both had worked their crews into a high state of efficiency. *Constitution* and *United States* each achieved around 100 hits in their frigate battles, and as a result both reduced their opponents to wrecks in just 30 minutes. No fewer than 30 of *Constitution*'s hits penetrated below *Java*'s waterline, creating leaks that could not be plugged.

Constitution had been at sea for eight weeks when it met *Java*. During that period, Bainbridge had drilled his gun crews constantly with both blank-firing and target practice. In the six weeks Lambert had been at sea before the battle, he conducted just six blank-firing practice exercises.

American gunnery at its worst was still good. The inexperienced *Chesapeake* fired 260 to 300 rounds during the ten-minute gunnery duel, and 50 of these shots – nearly 20 percent – struck home. Given the woeful standard of gunnery aboard *Guerrière* and *Macedonian*, Hull and Decatur would still have defeated their opponents if they had been commanding *Chesapeake* instead of a Humphreys 44 (assuming the crew was at the same level of training that *Constitution* and *United States* were). Lawrence possibly could have, even with the scratch crew he had on *Chesapeake*.

Against Broke and *Shannon*, Lawrence stood no chance. *Shannon* matched *Chesapeake*'s 20 percent hit rate while firing 30 percent faster. Additionally, the well-drilled crew of *Shannon* (it had been in commission since 1806) was not nearly as brittle as that of *Chesapeake*. Despite casualties that proved devastating to other British frigates, the crew of *Shannon* stood by their guns. Meanwhile, confusion reigned on *Chesapeake*.

Boarding decided only one of the four actions, although in two others boarding parties were called, but never fought. Despite what is read in naval fiction, by 1812 boarding was an act of desperation. Dacres and Chads only attempted to take *Constitution* by boarding because the ships they commanded were unmanageable, and boarding offered the sole opportunity for victory. In both battles, prompt responses from *Constitution*'s crew delayed the British boarding parties until *Constitution* broke contact with the British frigate.

Only Broke successfully boarded an opponent. That was due to a unique set of circumstances, combined with Broke's recognition of the opportunity. Broke recognized that the confusion on *Chesapeake*'s quarterdeck would allow a small party to gain control of the spar deck. With the spar deck under enemy control, the sailors on the gun deck would be forced to surrender. He acted quickly, and fortune rewarded his measured boldness with victory, albeit at the price of a disabling injury.

The potential boarding actions underscored one important point. While a ship's carronades and long guns could cause massive casualties, musketry was equally deadly at close range. For officers, it was musketry that was the deadlier threat. Table 2 shows casualties suffered during these four battles.

One battle, between *United States* and *Macedonian*, was primarily a long-range gunnery duel. The distribution of casualties by rank were roughly proportionate to the composition of the crews. Six percent of a ship's complement are typically commissioned and warrant officers, and these officers accounted for eight percent of the American casualties and two percent of British casualties. Since great guns are aimed at a ship, rather than an individual, this is what would be expected if casualties occurred purely randomly.

Many casualties were caused by marksmen, here pictured in one of the ship's fighting tops. Officers, including the warrant officers, were easily identified because they wore uniforms, and were often targeted. Killing a ship's officers left it leaderless, and easier prey. (AC)

Table 2: Casualties by Rank

Ship	Crew size		Killed or mortally wounded		Injured	
	Officers	Men	Officers	Men	Officers	Men
Constitution	27	429	1	6	2	5
Guerrière	18	254	1	22	6	50
United States	27	451	1	6	0	5
Macedonian	18	283	0	43	2	59
Constitution	27	440	9*		26*	
Java	426*		48*		102*	
Chesapeake	24	355	9	52	8	77
Shannon	18	312	3	30	3	47

* Neither dispatch broke casualties down by rank. Additionally, the number of supernumeraries aboard *Java* makes it difficult to determine the number of officers aboard.

The number of casualties increases significantly once ships come within musket range. While some of this could be attributed to a greater percentage of cannon fire hitting, the distribution of casualties also shifts once marksmen start to play a part in the battle. In the battle between *Constitution* and *Guerrière*, 21 percent of the American and ten percent of the British casualties were officers.

Disdaining an opportunity to rake his foe, Lawrence chose instead to battle yardarm-to-yardarm, a maneuver which allowed *Shannon*'s superior gunnery to hit his ship hard. Here, *Chesapeake* is shown approaching *Shannon*, while Broke backs sail to avoid being raked. (LOC)

On *Chesapeake* and *Shannon*, 12 percent of American and six percent of the British casualties were officers. Over 70 percent of the American officers aboard *Chesapeake* were killed or wounded, including the captain and every lieutenant. The few who were spared included the warrant officers stationed safely below the waterline: the surgeon in the cockpit and the gunner in his magazine. Aboard the victorious *Shannon*, a quarter of its officers were casualties.

From the marksmen's positions in the fighting tops and along the bulwarks, the enemy officers were easy to identify. Only officers and marines wore uniforms in the navies of 1812, and marine uniforms differed radically from those of naval officers. Marksmen knew that depriving a ship of its leadership was one of the most effective ways of demoralizing its crew, and targeted their fire accordingly. Once a ship came within musket range, therefore, casualties followed the old sailor's toast. They were distributed like prize money – the lion's share to the officers.

Captains suffered the most. Of eight captains in these four duels, two were killed and three wounded. The fortune of battle also took a high toll on masters, and first lieutenants suffered almost as much as captains, with one killed and four wounded. All of these officers were stationed on the quarterdeck, the most exposed position on a warship, in order to manage the ship. The price of glory was often paid in blood.

A final point bears emphasis. For a naval officer, combat at sea was rare. Most of his career consisted of dreary blockade duty, chasing down privateers or enemy merchantmen, or escorting convoys. An average sea officer might see action once every few years, and would generally be lucky to command a ship in one battle. One whose career started in 1793 and continued until 1816 would have had an unusually active career if he had been involved in as few as a dozen major engagements, including single-ship duels and fleet actions.

AFTERMATH

The fight between *Chesapeake* and *Shannon* was the last frigate duel of the war. Except for *Essex*, loose in the south Pacific, American frigates remained bottled up in port through the rest of 1813 and most of 1814. When American frigates did take to sea, they were hunted by Royal Navy squadrons, rather than meeting British frigates in single combat.

A treaty ending the War of 1812 was signed in Ghent, Belgium on Christmas Eve, 1814, but due to the speed of oceanic travel it did not reach the United States until February. Britain and the United States were now both tired of fighting. With Napoleon

Constitution survived both the American Civil War, which destroyed sister frigate *United States*, and late-nineteenth century neglect. Restored in the twentieth century to its War of 1812 appearance, *Constitution* is shown under sail on the bicentennial of its launch, in 1997. (US Navy photo)

Macedonian was kept as a prize for many years by the US Navy. Its figurehead is preserved at the United States Naval Academy (USNAM)

defeated, Britain no longer had any need for impressment or trade restrictions. Canada had proved indigestible to the United States. War was expensive and interfered with mutually profitable trade between the two nations. The treaty settled the war on the basis of *status quo ante bellum*, and remained silent on impressment. Territory captured by both sides was returned. The war had changed amost nothing.

Between the treaty's signing and its ratification, the war went on. A bloody battle was fought at New Orleans, which secured the reputation of General Andrew Jackson. The frigate USS *President* was caught slipping out of New York harbor and taken by HMS *Endymion* after another fierce battle. It was not a really a single-ship duel, because *Endymion* was accompanied by a British frigate squadron. But even after peace was formally established, it took time for word to get out. *Constitution* fought its last battle three days after Congress signed the treaty, taking a legitimate prize, HMS *Cyane*, which thereafter served in the US Navy.

The surviving captains – both victorious and vanquished – went on to distinguished careers within their navies, and into legend. Bainbridge commanded an American expedition against the Barbary States in 1815, and Hull joined the United States Navy Board. Dacres went on to become an admiral, commanding the Cape of Good Hope in 1845.

Chesapeake, *Shannon*, and *President* were all so badly damaged that they spent most of the rest of their careers in harbor, as receiving ships or stores ships. However, the Royal Navy did *President* the compliment of building a new frigate to its lines. Also christened HMS *President*, it had a long career, fighting in the Pacific during the Crimean War of the 1850s.

Shannon was reduced to a hulk in 1831 and broken up in 1859. By then, its most famous adversary had already been sold, broken up and its timbers used to construct a mill in Wickham, Hampshire. The mill, known as Chesapeake Mill, still exists and is now an antiques shop. *Macedonian* served as a frigate in the US Navy for another 13 years after the War of 1812 ended, finally being scrapped in 1828. As with *President*, the US Navy preserved its memory with a replacement.

The new ship, also named *Macedonian*, was larger than its namesake, but the US Navy deliberately retained the upper appearance of the old ship, even transferring the original figurehead. This second *Macedonian* remained in the navy until 1877. When it was sold out of the service the old figurehead was saved, and it now sits on the grounds of the United States Naval Academy.

The *United States* had the ill-fortune to be at the Norfolk Naval Yard at the start of the American Civil War. The yard was taken and recaptured during that war, and in the course of hostilities the old frigate was burned. *Constitution*, a fortunate ship, survived the Civil War and neglect in the late nineteenth century, and at the start of the twentieth century was restored to its former glory. It has remained a museum ship ever since. In the 1990s *Constitution* underwent a further refit, and on its bicentennial once again sailed under its own power.

FURTHER READING

There has been much ink spilled on the naval battles of the War of 1812. Much was wasted – if accuracy is more important than drama. A partial listing of my sources is given below. These works are the most accurate and relevant to a modern reader without access to research libraries. I also used my personal collection of nineteenth-century histories for many of the illustrations.

For accounts of the battle I used two major sources, William James and Theodore Roosevelt, supplemented by some modern histories. (Gardiner's *Naval War of 1812* is representative.) James is a major mythmaker, strongly prejudiced against the United States, but is authoritative on European navies. Read with caution, he is invaluable, especially when balanced by Roosevelt's account.

For seamanship of the era, you cannot do better than Harland's work, or a modern reprint of Brady's manual.

Chapelle and Caney hold the palms on American shipbuilding, Gardiner and Goodwin on British naval architecture. The "Anatomy of the Ship" series, two of which are listed below, is also invaluable.

Howard Douglas is an indispensable on naval gunnery, and is available in facsimile reprints.

For fictional accounts, look for Jon Williams' long out-of-print and thoroughly delightful "Privateers and Gentlemen" series. The last three books in the series: *The Raider*, *The Macedonian*, and *Cat Island*, relate the fictional history of Favian Marham, USN, in entertaining and historically accurate prose (except for the fictional characters).

Patrick O'Brian hardly needs introduction, and is also entertaining and accurate. The same is true of C. S. Forester, although Horatio Hornblower spent 1812 in the Baltic. Forester's lessser-known *Captain from Connecticut* centers around a War of 1812 frigate duel with an unusual conclusion.

United States was a popular command into the late 1840s. Unfortunately it was at Gosport Naval Yard in Norfolk, Virginia, when the Civil War erupted. Although it avoided destruction when the Union abandoned and burned the base in 1861, it was burned by retreating Confederates when the base was retaken in 1862. (AC)

Brady, William, *The Kedge-Anchor, or Young Sailors' Assistant*, W Brady, New York, 1847

Caney, Donald L., *Sailing Warships of the US Navy*, US Naval Institute Press, Annapolis, MD, 2001

Chapelle, Howard I., *The History of the American Sailing Navy*, W. W. Norton, New York, 1949

De Kay, James T., *Chronicles of the Frigate Macedonian, 1809–1922*, W. W. Norton & Company, New York, 1995

Douglas, Howard, *A Treatise on Naval Gunnery*, 2nd ed., John Murray, London, 1829

Dudley, William S., ed., *The Naval War of 1812, A Documentary History*, (three vols) Naval Historical Center, Department of the Navy, Washington, 1965,

Gardiner, Robert, *The Naval War of 1812*, Chatham Publishers, 1998

Gardiner, Robert, *Frigates of the Napoleonic Wars*, United States Naval Institute Press, Annapolis, 2000

Goodwin, Peter, *Construction and Fitting of the English Man of War 1650–1850*, Conway Maritime Press Ltd, London, 1987

Harland, John, *Seamanship in the Age of Sail*, US Naval Institute Press, Annapolis, MD, 1990

James, William, *The Naval History of Great Britain, from the Declaration of War by France in 1793, to the Accession of George IV*, Richard Bentley, London, 1859

Marquardt, Karl Heinz, *The 44-Gun Frigate USS Constitution, "Old Ironsides,"* US Naval Institute Press, Annapolis, MD, 2005

An allegorical painting of the Treaty of Ghent, ending the War of 1812. Britannia and Columbia shake hands as they hold olive branches. Behind them, two sailors hold national flags and a white banner of truce. (LOC)

Mooney, James L., ed., *The Dictionary of American Naval Fighting Ships*, US Government Printing Office, Washington, 1977

Moore, Sir Alan, *Sailing Ships of War, 1800–1860*, Halton and Truscott Smith, Ltd., London, 1926

Roosevelt, Theodore, *The Naval War of 1812*, G. P. Putnam's Sons, New York and London, 1900

White, David, *The Frigate Diana*, Conway Maritime Press Ltd, London, 1987

GLOSSARY

Backing (a sail):	Pivoting the spar on which a sail is hung so that the sail is being blown backwards, against the mast.
Beating:	Sailing in the direction of the wind, at an angle to it. The sails act as an airfoil, pulling the ship ahead, but reaching a position dead to windward required a ship to follow a zig-zag course. Most square-rigged ships could sail no closer than 40 degrees from the direction the wind was blowing, but fore-and-aft rigs could sail closer.
Bowsprit:	A spar projecting forward from the bow of the ship, to which the stays on the lower sections of the foremast attach.
Broad reaching:	Sailing with the wind from behind and to the side. A sailing ship was fastest while broad reaching, because all of the sails were being pushed by the wind.
Course:	The lowest square sail, hung from a spar set on the lower mast.
Fore-and-aft sails:	Triangular and trapezoidal sails that were rigged parallel to the length of the ship. The sails set on the stays that supported the masts were called staysails or jibsails (if they were on the jib stays). The sail set on a gaff and boom attached behind the mizzenmast was called the gaff, spanker or spencer sail, depending on the navy, period and rig. Fore-and-aft sails were used to help steer the ship, and when beating into the wind.
Foremast:	On a full-rigged ship, or a brig, the foremost mast.
Jib boom:	A pole or spar extending from the bowsprit.
Jib sails:	Triangular sails hung from stays running from the upper foremasts to the jib boom. Used to help steer the ship.
Lee-gage:	The position downwind of the enemy ship.

Leeward:	The side opposite to the direction of the wind.
Royal sail:	A square sail above the topgallant sail. On most ships, the royal was set on a spar on the topgallant mast above the topgallant sail. This is called a "flying" royal. On larger frigates, especially United States frigates, the royal would be mounted on a separate royal mast, attached to the top of the topgallant mast.
Running:	Sailing with the wind directly behind the ship. It is the easiest way to sail a square-rigged ship, but slower than broad reaching, because the after sails blanket sails mounted on masts ahead of them.
Ship-rigged:	A ship with at least three masts, all carrying square sails, is said to be ship-rigged.
Shroud:	A line running from the sides of the ship to the top of the lower mast, or from the mast top platform or crosstrees to the top of the section of the mast. They are used to guy the mast.
Spanker, spencer, or mizzen gaffsail:	A trapezoidal sail mounted aft of the mizzen mast, used to help handle the ship. Spankers and Spencers have booms holding the bottom of the sail. Gaffsails often do not. These are called "loose-footed gaffs."
Squaresail:	Four-sided sails, occasionally square, but more often trapezoidal, set on spars. American frigates generally mounted five, and sometimes six, sails on their masts. From lowest to highest were the course, topsail, topgallant, royal, skysail, and moonsail or hope-in-heaven. (The name of the sixth sail varied widely.)
Stay	A line from the top of a mast to the ship, keeping the mast in position. They either run to the side of the ship, to the next mast, or to the bowsprit and jib boom. The stays that run forward are called stays. The ones running aft to the sides of the ship are called backstays.
Studding (or stun) sails:	Sails mounted outboard the square sails to add more sail area during light and moderate winds.
Tack:	(in reference to a maneuver) To tack a ship is to turn the ship into the wind such that the bow of the ship moves across the direction from which the wind is blowing.
Tack:	(in reference to a course being steered) A ship is said to be on a starboard tack if the wind is coming from the right side of ship. It is on a larboard (or port) if the wind is coming from the left.
Topgallant sail:	The sail above the topsail. At this period it was carried on a separate mast, called a topgallant mast, attached to the top of the topmast.
Topsail:	The sail on a mast above the course. At this period, it was carried on its own section of mast, called the topmast.
Weather-gage:	The position upwind of the enemy ship.
Wear:	To turn the ship away from the direction the wind is blowing. This puts less strain on the masts and rigging than tacking (turning into the direction of the wind). Now generally called gybing or jibing.
Windward:	The side from which the wind is coming.

INDEX